The
Parent's
Guide to
Your Child and Food

The **ParenTalk** Guide to Your Child and Food

Dr Derrick Cutting

Series Editor: Steve Chalke

Illustrated by John Byrne

Hodder & Stoughton
LONDON SYDNEY AUCKLAND

British Library Cataloguing in Publication Data
A record for this book is available from the British Library

ISBN 0 340 78540 3

Typeset by Avon Dataset Ltd, Bidford-on-Avon, Warks

Printed and bound in Great Britain by
Clays Ltd, St Ives plc

Hodder and Stoughton
A Division of Hodder Headline Ltd
338 Euston Road
London NW1 3BH

Contents

PART ONE: DIETETICS FOR DUMMIES

Sam's Tea

What Children Are Eating Today

'Here's your tea, darling,' said Mum, placing the plate carefully on the little table in front of Sam as he watched TV. 'I'll get your drink.'

For a moment, Mum thought there was a flicker of response in Sam's eyes, but it was probably just a reflection of the TV screen. Certainly he didn't look down at the plate as he felt for his fork. He didn't need to. He knew what was on it: chicken nuggets, chips and crisps. Mum fetched the cup of cola to wash it down.

At five o'clock, every day, this is what Sam had for tea. Well, sometimes he would have fizzy orange or lemon to drink, but Mum had given up surprising him with food. She knew that anything green would be rejected (unless it was artificially coloured sugar and gelatine, preferably shaped like a snake). Bit by bit, the familiar food found its way to Sam's mouth, but never once distracted him from his TV programme.

Meanwhile, Mum tidied the kitchen, loaded the washing machine, scraped chocolate off the computer and rescued Sam's soldiers from the hamster cage. Dad would be home in an hour. Once Sam was in bed, Mum and Dad would enjoy an evening meal together. She searched the kitchen cupboard for inspiration. What should she cook this evening? Oh yes. She had tomatoes, tuna, onions and herbs – just what she needed to knock up a quick pasta bake. The pasta shells were getting low, so she added them to her shopping list and, while she thought of it, she added oven-ready chips and chicken nuggets too; she had nightmares about going to the freezer and finding she'd run out of food for Sam.

'Mum, can I have my chocolate biscuit now?' called Sam.

'Yes,' replied Mum. 'I'm just coming.'

Reaching for the biscuit tin, Mum had her usual doubts about whether Sam was eating the right things. But she told herself that you can only feed children what they'll eat. And most children these days eat much the same as Sam – don't they?

So What?

So kids don't eat the best foods. What does it matter? After all, you're only young once. You have the rest of your life to develop more sophisticated tastes. And why burden our children with worries about heart disease and cancer? How many children have heart attacks?

The alarming truth is that many adult diseases begin in childhood. Coronary heart disease – our number one killer – results from fatty deposits building up in arteries. These fatty deposits start forming in pre-school children! Recent research supports the view that conditions such as high blood pressure, raised cholesterol, diabetes and heart disease in adults are influenced by nutrition in infancy – and even in the womb!

We have an epidemic of obesity in the Western world, with up to half of adults being overweight, and the problem is getting worse. It's an increasing problem in children too. And fat children are likely to become fat adults. You can spend a lifetime struggling with faulty food habits developed in childhood.

Of course, if your children eat well, they won't have to wait until adult life to reap the benefits: they will be healthier children.

 Top Tip: *Learning to eat well now can protect your child from future disease.*

Health depends on good nutrition. Food is our fuel. But there's a lot more to food than that. I'm glad we don't go to a filling station to get a balanced blend of nutrients, delivered through a pipe. Food is fun. Sam had no idea what he was missing. Food deserves our full attention; it doesn't get it when we're transfixed by the TV.

We don't arrive in this world as gurgling gourmets. Learning to appreciate good food is part of growing up. You can't expect children to suddenly start eating well when they reach eighteen if they've never learnt how. Would you spontaneously give a virtuoso piano recital if you'd only learnt the recorder?

FOOD DESERVES OUR FULL ATTENTION

Why Should the Grown-ups Get All the Good Grub?

Perhaps your children, like Sam, eat separately from the adults in your household. This is very common these days. Sometimes it's hard to get everyone in the family to meet up long enough to say 'hello', let alone eat a meal together.

So it's convenient to buy ready-made items such as chicken nuggets, sausage rolls, burgers and chips which take only a few moments to transfer from the freezer to the oven. These are easily supplemented with snack foods – such as crisps, biscuits and cakes – which come in handy packets.

Finding time to prepare a decent meal for the adults isn't easy. No wonder we buy fast food for the children.

Indeed, a curious custom has emerged in our society. We no

4

longer feed our children normal food. Instead, we feed them special stuff called 'kids' food'. When it's dinosaur-shaped, it's clearly aimed at children (or possibly palaeontologists).

The food industry uses a range of ploys to target children. Once your child has spotted the cartoon on the carton, you can find yourself fighting for the right to buy another brand of yoghurt. And, of course, you have to keep buying those Sugar Pops until the full set of plastic monsters is collected. Shameless TV adverts interrupt children's programmes to convince your child that life is pointless without the latest cartoon cakes or dinosaur dippers.

It wouldn't be so bad if these children's foods were of the right quality. Sadly, all too often, inside that attractive packaging lurks a highly processed product – loaded with fat, salt, sugar and additives.

It may be that you're trying to eat wisely yourself but, like Sam's mum, you feel forced to feed your child 'junk'. If you didn't care, you probably wouldn't be reading this book. Here's some great news: you do have a choice! And, with a little knowledge and patience, you can help your child to love good food.

Sugar and Spice and All Things Nice

We Are What We Eat: Food Facts

We know what little girls are made of, but what about the food they eat? What's food made of?

Food is made up of four important groups of nutrients:

1. protein;
2. carbohydrate;
3. fat;
4. vitamins and minerals.

1. Protein

A lot of important structures in our bodies are made of proteins. Children need protein for growth and we all need it for the body's repair programme. Proteins are made up of smaller molecules called amino acids. When you eat protein, your digestive system breaks it down into amino acids which are absorbed into the bloodstream and used to build new proteins.

What are essential amino acids?

The body can also make some amino acids. Other amino acids, which the body is unable to manufacture, are called 'essential amino acids' and these must be obtained from food.

Protein from animal sources (such as meat, poultry, fish, milk, and eggs) contains adequate amounts of these essential amino acids; this is called high biological value (HBV) protein. Most of the protein supplied by plant foods (such as rice, peas and maize) is short on one or two essential amino acids and is known as low biological value (LBV) protein.

When I was working in a remote part of rural South Africa, I used to see children with kwashiorkor (a serious illness caused by protein deficiency). Instead of breast milk, some children were given a food made of ground-up maize. It looked nourishing enough, but it didn't contain all the necessary amino acids; the consequences were catastrophic.

Will my child get enough protein on a vegan diet?

If you're a vegan, relying on plants to supply all your protein, don't panic! As long as a good variety of plant foods is included, and pulses are combined with cereals (e.g. beans on toast, peas with rice, lentils with pasta), you needn't go short of any amino acids. Even so, if you want to give a vegan diet to children, you must be extra careful to provide adequate protein, calories, and vitamin B_{12}. (Deficiency of vitamin B_{12} in babies can cause serious problems – see page 35.) Soya beans are particularly useful because, like animal products, they provide HBV protein.

 Top Tip: *Make sure your child has a good intake of protein every day – whether from animal sources or plants.*

Children and adults eating a typical Western diet get more than enough protein.

2. Carbohydrate

Carbohydrates are important energy foods. As their name suggests, they are made from nothing but carbon and the elements of water (hydrogen and oxygen).

Sugars, starches and fibre are all forms of carbohydrate.

Sugar
Sugars are *simple carbohydrates*. They occur naturally in fruit and vegetables. We enjoy their sweet taste. You needn't be concerned about the natural sugar content of food, but it can lead to problems when refined sugar, extracted from the sugar cane, is added to food and drink.

Adding sugar to food adds 'empty calories' – calories without nourishment or fibre. Excessive sugar intake is bad for the teeth, and may contribute to obesity and diabetes.

9

You can see the sugar in your sugar bowl, and count the spoonfuls if you put it in your tea, but you may not realise the can of soft drink you are giving your child contains *seven* teaspoons of sugar. Obviously, sweets, cakes, biscuits, puddings, jellies and some yoghurts are packed with sugar. But look out for the sugar added to savoury foods like baked beans and canned sweetcorn.

Don't be duped into thinking that honey or brown sugar are much better for your child than white sugar. In fact, honey, sucrose, maltose, lactose, fructose, glucose, glucose syrup, dextrose, invert sugar and caramel are all variations on the same theme – sugar.

Because so much is hidden in processed food and drink, you would probably be horrified if you could see all the sugar your child is consuming. Here are ten ways to cut down your child's sugar intake:

1. Use more unprocessed food, e.g. fresh fruit and vegetables.
2. If you buy tinned fruit, choose fruit in natural juice – not syrup.
3. Read food labels; choose the can of sweetcorn without added sugar.
4. Serve fewer sweet foods: even artificial sweetening encourages a liking for sugar.
5. When cooking, don't add unnecessary sugar. If your child has already developed a sweet tooth, cut down gradually.
6. Dried fruits – such as raisins, sultanas, dates, figs, prunes and apricots – can be used to sweeten home-made cakes and biscuits.
7. Choose low-sugar breakfast cereals and top with chopped banana or dried fruit.

8. Buy (or make) jams or fruit spreads with a reduced sugar content and keep them in the fridge once opened.
9. Give plain water as a drink from an early age. If your child is already in the habit of drinking heavily sweetened juice/squash, gradually add less and less flavouring.
10. Use a variety of chopped fruits to replace sweet puddings.

Starch

Starches are *complex carbohydrates* – made up from lots of sugar units (glucose) joined together. Cereals (e.g. wheat and rice), foods made from cereal grains (e.g. bread and pasta), and root vegetables (e.g. potatoes and parsnips) are loaded with starch. These foods supply energy along with other nutrients and fibre, all conveniently packaged within the whole grain or vegetable.

 Top Tip: *Give your child more whole grains and less sugar (which is often hidden in processed foods).*

You may have been taught, perhaps by a rather starchy schoolteacher, that these foods are fattening. There is only a grain of truth in this: in the end, eating too much of any food that supplies energy could make you fat if you didn't use up the calories.

In fact, though, eating plenty of these starchy foods in their natural form is much less likely to make you or your child fat than eating highly processed convenience foods. They provide energy with bulk, so you don't take in too many calories before

11

your stomach fills up and you feel satisfied. As a rule, starchy foods keep hunger at bay better than fatty foods. Also, in general, the energy is released more slowly than it is from a sudden dose of refined sugar; this is better for your child's metabolism.

Indeed, there is currently a great deal of scientific interest in this very point. When starch is digested, it is broken down into sugar units and absorbed as glucose into the bloodstream. Some foods cause a rapid rise in blood glucose, while others give up their glucose more slowly. Foods can be given a GI number. This is nothing to do with American soldiers (although it may have important implications for the performance of armed forces). It stands for 'glycaemic index'.

Pure glucose is given a GI of 100; it's absorbed immediately, causing a rapid rise in blood glucose. A food producing only half this glucose response has a GI of 50. The lower the GI number, the more slowly glucose is released from the food. Table 1 shows the GI numbers for a few common foods.

We know that people with diabetes are better off eating more of the lower GI foods in place of those that cause a bigger rise in blood glucose. It may be that other people are less likely to develop diabetes, weight problems and heart disease if they do the same.

Basmati rice has a lower GI than instant rice; new potatoes have a lower GI than baked potatoes; apples, pears and plums have lower GIs than tropical fruits such as melons and pineapples. In general, pulses (peas, beans, lentils) and pastas have lovely low GI numbers.

When choosing foods for your child, you needn't worry about the glycaemic index. The important thing is to use as much whole, natural, unprocessed food as possible. When you

Table 1

GI Numbers of Some Common Foods

Food	Glycaemic Index
Breakfast cereals	
Porridge	42
Shredded Wheat	67
Cornflakes	84
Rice	
Basmati	58
Instant (boiled 6 min.)	90
Bread	
Mixed grain	40–50
Pitta	57
Wholemeal	69
White	70
Baguette	95
Pasta	
Vermicelli	35
Spaghetti	41
Macaroni	45
Potatoes	
New	62
Baked	85

Food	Glycaemic Index
Pulses	
Soya beans	18
Peas – dried (boiled)	22
Kidney beans	27
Lentils	26–30
Chickpeas	33
Haricot beans	38
Blackeye beans	42
Peas – frozen (boiled)	48
Baked beans	48
Fruit	
Cherries	22
Grapefruit	25
Pear	37
Plum	39
Apple	32–40
Orange	44
Grapes	46
Banana	54
Mango	56
Raisins	64
Pineapple	66
Watermelon	72

This scale is based on tests comparing the blood glucose response to swallowing 50 g of glucose with the response to 50 g of carbohydrate from other foods. Glucose is given a value of 100; the blood glucose response to white bread is 70 per cent of this so it has a GI of 70.

The trouble is, people don't like taking 50 g of glucose so some studies have used white bread as the standard instead. Confusingly, this has resulted in a second GI scale in which white bread has a value of 100. You can easily convert from one scale to the other by applying the ratio 7:10 – as long as you know which scale you're dealing with!

do buy processed food such as bread and breakfast cereals, try to include those that use whole grains. Recent research confirms that wholegrain foods can help to protect against heart disease and cancer. Cereal grains are naturally packed with a balanced blend of micronutrients. Why let the food manufacturer mess them about before giving them to your child?

Just as refined sugar has been separated from all naturally occurring nutrients, starch too can be stripped to leave nothing but naked calories. When there is such a variety of whole, natural foods, it goes against the grain to buy too many processed products padded out with this 'modified starch', which you will often see on food labels – even on baby foods.

Fibre

Fibre, which was once called 'roughage', is also in the *complex carbohydrate* group. It's the part of fruits, vegetables and cereals that supplies us with natural sugars and starches. As we can't digest it, it may seem to be unnecessary. After all, it's just the dross that's left behind after the intestine has extracted all the goodness. The food industry 'helpfully' removes fibre to give us white bread, white rice, cornflakes and fruit juice.

I know a little girl who thought her brother's nappies would fit better without all the bulky stuffing. It soon became clear she was wrong! In the same way, the discarded fibre has turned out to be important. In fact, the lack of fibre in Western diets may go a long way towards explaining why many medical problems (including constipation, diverticular disease, acute appendicitis, bowel cancer and gallstones) are so common here yet so rare in some other parts of the world (e.g. rural Africa).

There are two main types of fibre. *Insoluble fibre* – obtained from vegetables (including the skins) and cereal husks – helps the bowels to work properly and allows you to feel satisfied without eating too many calories. *Soluble fibre* – from fruits, vegetables, pulses and oats – helps to lower blood cholesterol and to slow down the release of glucose from starchy foods.

If you use wholegrain cereals and unprocessed fruit and vegetables your child will not go short of fibre. It is not generally necessary to add extra bran to food and doing so can reduce the absorption of certain minerals.

While most adults would benefit from eating more fibre, it is important not to overload young children with high-fibre foods such as wholemeal bread and pulses – especially in the first two years. Babies and toddlers have immature digestive systems. They have small stomachs and big energy requirements. Too much fibre will fill them up before they've taken in enough calories. The mistake of applying adult guidelines to infants gave rise to so-called 'muesli-belt malnutrition'.

> **Top Tip:** Your child needs fibre from fruit, pulses and whole grains – but don't overdo it in the first two years.

3. Fat

> Jack Sprat could eat no fat,
> His wife could eat no lean;
> And so, between them both, you see,
> They licked the platter clean.

Fat is a high-energy fuel. The calorie rating of food is just a measure of the heat energy released when it is used as fuel. Weight for weight, fat contains more than double the calories of protein, sugar or starch (and now you know why candles aren't made of potato).

Our bodies use fat to store energy, and this may be evident on a bottom or belly near you. When we eat more calories than we use up, our bodies save the surplus fuel as fat – a biological cushion against unsuccessful hunting, crop failure or millennium bugs. It's just as well we don't store spare calories as starch or we would end up bigger, heavier and probably very stiff.

Every gram of fat you eat supplies you with 9 calories (or, more correctly, kilocalories) compared with only 4 calories from a gram of protein or sugar. Most adults in the West would benefit from eating far less fat, not only to control body weight but also to avoid developing heart disease.

In a typical UK diet, about 40 per cent of the calories come

17

from fat. You would be better off getting less than 30 per cent of your calories that way. Perhaps you're thinking, 'I don't eat anything like that much fat!' But, as we've seen, fat is 'energy-dense': a little fat means a lot of calories. And most of the fat we eat is hidden. Many meals with no visible fat will push you over the 30 per cent mark before you can say 'Jack Sprat'.

Should I give my child a low-fat diet?

Babies are not miniature adults! They need to take in about 50 per cent of their energy as fat. Breast or formula milk will supply their needs in the first few months. Don't use reduced-fat milks or attempt to introduce a low-fat diet in the first two years. After that, semi-skimmed milk can be brought in.

Your aim is, very gently, to ease your toddler from dependence on a relatively high-fat diet towards a more grown-up way of eating. Joining in family meals helps. By the age of five it is ideal for a child to sit down regularly with adults and share the same food. Schoolchildren, like adults, should get no more than a third of their calories from fat.

How can I cut down the family's fat intake?

The problem is that so many processed foods, including those aimed at children, harbour heaps of hidden fat. Try not to make too much use of sausages, burgers and other processed meats; pies and pastries; and products with a crispy coating such as fish fingers and chicken nuggets: they all conceal alarming quantities of unhelpful fat.

Top Tip: *Cut back on the family fat intake, but give your child full-fat products for the first two years.*

When you buy convenience foods, have a look at the nutritional information panel; it's generally helpful to go for those with no more than 5 grams of fat per 100 grams.

Of course, the way you cook food makes a big difference to the amount of fat that ends up on the plate (and in your child's tummy). There's very little fat in a potato, but if you chop it up and deep-fry it, the resulting chips are drenched in fat. A woman came to see me recently, very concerned that her daughter was overweight. She was trying to buy low-fat foods and was pleased to find some reduced-fat sausages; but it turned out she was frying them in lard – a fat lot of good!

You can be sure that sausages and other processed meat products will be packed with fat and salt (which are cheap ingredients) but what else is in them? No doubt 'mechanically recovered meat' won't be prime steak. How often do you have unidentified frying objects sizzling in your pan? Wouldn't you rather know what you're feeding your child? If you can't identify it, best not buy it.

Recognisable fish, chicken, turkey or red meat might seem more expensive but you can see what you're getting for your money. Skinless chicken and turkey breasts are convenient and low in fat; serving poultry with the skin can treble the fat content. Choose lean red meat and trim off visible fat.

Game for a gamble?

Game such as rabbit or venison will generally be less fatty than lamb, pork or beef. Frisky, frolicking animals are leaner than more sedentary residents of a farm (and anything from the ostrich to the kangaroo seems fair game these days). Your child may take to game, but there's a high risk of rejection if it's unfamiliar. As a small boy, I used to love my mother's rabbit stew (before I had a pet rabbit). A special offer may persuade you to try your luck. Slipping a little game meat into a familiar casserole might improve your chances of success, but you may still end up giving the game away.

Dairy products

A lot of the fat we eat comes from dairy products such as milk, cheese and butter. Once your child is five years old, it's a good idea to use skimmed milk – not only in food but also for drinks. It has all the calcium and protein of whole milk without the fat. Powdered skimmed milk is very convenient and is fortified with vitamins A and D; it can be mixed with water in a jug and, when refrigerated, you wouldn't know it hadn't come from a bottle.

For cooking, the change from whole milk to skimmed is easy: you're unlikely to get any complaints. For drinks and cereal, using whole milk one day and fully skimmed the next is asking for trouble. It's wise to let your child get used to semi-skimmed milk first; as the palate adapts, you can gradually increase the proportion of skimmed milk. As long as the blend is prepared out of sight and presented in a familiar container, the transition will be painless. (Perhaps your child is completely reasonable, but many will declare the milk 'disgusting' as soon as they catch you making a change.)

Eating Better on a Budget

Here are a few tips to help you look after the health of your family and your finances:

★ Eat plenty of low-cost, high-starch foods such as potatoes and wholegrain bread, pasta, rice and other cereals.

★ Use plenty of pulses (peas, beans, lentils) which are good sources of protein (when combined with cereals) and cost less than meat.

★ Add pulses to meat dishes (such as casseroles) to make a little meat go a long way.

★ Buy fruits and vegetables that are cheap at the time. Use the local market. But remember: it's no economy if it goes bad before you can eat it.

★ Buy foods on special offer. If powdered milk is half-price, buy the amount you will get through before the 'Use by' date. When fish fillets are cheaper, stock the freezer.

★ If possible, grow your own vegetables in the garden. Consider an allotment (if you know someone who likes digging).

Are there other ways of giving my child good protein without unwanted fat?
If you want a really low-fat source of protein, don't forget pulses like beans and lentils. It's good for your heart to get more protein from plants and less from animals. It can be good for your budget too: you can make a small amount of meat go a long way by adding lots of pulses. Protein from soya beans provides plenty of the essential amino acids making it a very good meat substitute. Tofu (soya bean curd), which takes up the flavour of other ingredients, can be used in all sorts of recipes.

Top Tip: *Getting more protein from plants and less from animals is good for your heart (and for animals).*

Quorn is another useful low-fat, high-protein meat substitute that will take on the flavour of any sauce you cook it in. It's made from a mushroom-like fungus and egg white. Your child may well approve of the chicken-like texture – as long as you get the flavour right!

Get your fats straight

'Fat's fat, and that's that,' said Jane, rejecting the pack of salmon steaks from her supermarket trolley. She picked up a pack of cod fillets and, seeing that the label showed much less fat per 100 grams than the label on salmon, she put it in her trolley.

Jane was following a low-fat diet. She was quite right that all types of fat are equally fattening (containing 9 kilocalories per gram). It's a fair bet that Jack Sprat had the profile of a beanpole while his wife resembled a bulging beanbag (the sort you sit on, I mean). But there's more to fat than that.

The nutritional information panel on packaged food tells you how much of the fat is in the form of 'saturates'. Sometimes you will also be informed about 'polyunsaturates' and 'mono-unsaturates'. What relevance does this have to a stressed parent, frantically throwing essential items into a supermarket trolley in a bid to reach the check-out before the children pass their 'Best before' time?

Clearly, you won't have long to linger over labels when the

Food Labels at a Glance

As a busy parent, you don't have time to linger over labels when you're shopping. You will generally want to buy products with a low content of salt, sugar and fat – particularly saturated fat (saturates). But what is low and what is high?

The food label tells you the number of grams (g) of sugar, fat and sodium in 100 g of the product. (1 g of sodium is 2.5 g of sodium chloride – i.e. common salt.) Here's a guide:

CONTENT PER 100 G OF PRODUCT

	A lot! (g)	A little! (g)
Sugar	10	2
Fat	20	3
– Saturates	5	1
Sodium	0.5	0.1

Here's a simple way to remember the figures for a low sugar and fat content that's easy as 1, 2, 3:

Saturated, Sugar is a Fat lot of good.

Of course, portion size is important too. Whole milk has only 4 g of fat per 100 g (so Farmer Giles can rightly claim that his milk is 96 per cent fat free). If you only sprinkled the occasional teaspoon of milk on your food, the amount of fat would be insignificant (and so would the supply of calcium). Because we get through a lot of milk, it's an important source of fat (and two-thirds of the fat is saturated).

children are with you. After reading this book, and spending a little time checking labels when you are not being harassed by children, you will be able to make good choices without looking at lots of labels during your regular shopping trip.

YOU WON'T HAVE LONG TO
LINGER OVER LABELS.

So where do those poly-thingummy-whatsits come in?

All fat is made up of a mixture of different 'fatty acids'. *Saturated* fatty acids (also called SFA or saturates) are the bad guys. We all have a fatty substance called cholesterol in the bloodstream, and when the cholesterol level is too high it can lead to a build-up of fatty deposits in arteries causing heart disease. Saturated fat pushes up blood cholesterol levels and can trigger the formation of blood clots in the circulation (thrombosis). Most of the saturated fat we eat comes from animals (e.g. red meat, processed meat, poultry, milk, butter, cream, cheese). But some plant foods contain a lot of saturates (e.g. coconut, coconut oil, palm oil). And fish, which are definitely animals and not plants, contain very little saturated fat.

Get Your Fats Straight

Type of Fat	Where Found	Advice
Mono-unsaturated	Olive oil, rapeseed oil, olive oil spread, almonds, hazelnuts, avocados	First choice
Polyunsaturated	Sunflower oil, corn oil, soya oil, safflower oil, sunflower spread, sunflower seeds	Second choice
Saturated	Palm oil, coconut oil, meat products (e.g. sausages, pies), full-fat dairy products, lard, dripping, suet, ghee	Avoid
Trans	Hydrogenated vegetable oil – a common ingredient in processed foods and hard margarines	Avoid

Children who eat a typical Western diet, with its high saturated fat content, begin to develop fatty deposits in their arteries before they start school. The long run-up to angina, a heart attack, or a stroke has begun. Communities that eat very little saturated fat don't have this problem.

Polyunsaturated fatty acids (PUFA, polyunsaturates) are more useful; they can lower blood cholesterol a little. Mind you, as well as lowering harmful cholesterol (LDL-cholesterol), huge doses of polyunsaturated fat can also lower helpful cholesterol (HDL-cholesterol). Remember, too, that poly-unsaturated fat is just as fattening as saturated fat. Replacing saturated fats with *a little* of those 'high in polyunsaturates' (e.g. sunflower spread, sunflower oil, corn oil) is a good move; piling on the polyunsaturates is not.

Fish contains special polyunsaturates called n-3 (or omega-3) fatty acids which can help to prevent blood clots and abnormal heart rhythms. Oily fish (such as salmon, sardines, pilchards, herring and mackerel) have higher levels of these n-3 fatty acids than white fish (such as cod, haddock, whiting and plaice). But all fish have very low levels of saturated fat and are great sources of protein. Try to put fish on the menu twice a week or more. If your child rejects fish at first, it's usually possible to find a couple of recipes that are acceptable (see pages 176–80).

Mono-unsaturated fatty acids (MUFA, mono-unsaturates) are fairly friendly fellows. When they replace saturated fat, there is a helpful drop in cholesterol (but beneficial HDL-cholesterol is not reduced).

 Top Tip: Saturated fat is bad for you and your child; mono-unsaturates are more friendly.

Olive oil is about 70 per cent mono-unsaturates and this may be one reason why people in Mediterranean countries suffer less heart disease than Northern Europeans. But it must be remembered that, apart from the use of olive oil, Mediterranean cuisine has a number of other helpful features. For example, there is a healthy emphasis on fruit, vegetables and fish.

Other rich sources of mono-unsaturates are rapeseed oil, avocados, hazelnuts, and almonds.

Don't forget that these mild mono-unsaturates are just as fattening as sinister saturates. Many a Greek has grown to a great girth on a Mediterranean diet. So, don't be too free with the olive oil – or you'll have a fat chance of controlling your waistline!

What about *trans* fatty acids? This is a term you won't often see on food labels, but – just like saturated fat – trans fat is something to avoid as much as possible. It's bad for cholesterol levels and bad for arteries. Trans fatty acids are formed during food processing when oils are 'hydrogenated' to make them thicker (e.g. in the production of margarines). Avoid hard margarines and try to reject processed foods in which 'hydrogenated vegetable oil' is near the top of the ingredients list.

Does it really matter which fats or cooking oils I use?

Knowing that fatty meats and processed meat products are full of saturated fat, you will be trying not to feature them too frequently on your child's menu. Instead, no doubt, you will be choosing: lean cuts of meat; pulses such as beans and lentils; fish; and skinless poultry. By doing so, you will be getting your child off to a good start in the battle against heart disease, obesity, diabetes, and cancer.

But if you add loads of saturated fat (or trans fat) when you cook or serve these foods, it won't help at all! So choose your cooking fats and spreading fats carefully.

Oils are better than fats, aren't they?

Fats that are liquid at room temperature are called oils and that certainly doesn't guarantee that they are good for you. Olive oil is a very fine first choice, but it is expensive. Extra virgin olive oil has a strong flavour; if your child likes the taste, you could use a little on salad – perhaps mixed with wine vinegar and ground pepper. When you don't want the strong taste, select 'light' olive oil: it has just as many calories but a lighter flavour.

Rapeseed oil (called 'canola oil' in USA) is cheaper than olive oil and is an excellent all-round oil – ideal for frying, baking or dressing salads. It doesn't have a strong flavour to offend a child's choosy palate. Like olive oil, rapeseed oil has a healthy level of mono-unsaturates, but it has a lower concentration of saturates than olive oil. There really is no need to have any other oil in your kitchen (you could even oil your hinges with it).

Top Tip: *Rapeseed oil is cheaper than olive oil and is an excellent all-round choice.*

Used sparingly, oils that are high in polyunsaturates (e.g. sunflower oil, safflower oil, soya oil and corn oil) are quite acceptable. For some recipes, you might like to experiment with interesting oils such as walnut oil or sesame seed oil.

Avoid palm oil and coconut oil which are full of saturated fat. Be wary of the term 'vegetable oil' in an ingredients' list: it could include palm or coconut oils. Mind you, blended vegetable oil is often a friendly combination of soya, rapeseed and corn oils, but it's as well to know what you're getting.

Try to avoid re-using oils after cooking: reheating can oxidise polyunsaturated fats, making them more damaging to arteries.

What about other fats for spreading and for cooking?

Lard, dripping, suet, and ghee are all packed with saturated fat. If you don't stock them, you won't use them – and you and

28

your child will be better for it. We have a local Indian restaurant that doesn't use any ghee at all now (only rapeseed oil). So it can be done.

Perhaps you have grown up feeling there's nothing quite like butter and that anything else you spread on your bread is second best. Over half the fat in butter is saturated so, if you want to carry on using it, spread it thinly. You would be better off switching to a reduced-fat spread with a high proportion of mono-unsaturates (as in olive oil) or polyunsaturates (as in sunflower oil). Believe it or not, your palate will soon adapt. If you give your child a reduced-fat spread made with olive oil from an early age, it will just be accepted as normal. Whether things taste right or not is simply a matter of habit.

The spreading fats containing plant stanols or sterols (such as Benecol and Flora pro.activ) may be useful for adults who need to lower their cholesterol levels; but they cost more than standard spreads and I wouldn't recommend them for children under five (except in families with inherited high cholesterol levels, on medical advice).

A very low-fat spread is fine on bread but unsuitable for cooking. However, a *reduced-fat* spread (59 per cent fat) can be used for frying, baking or roasting. Even so, for frying and roasting, rapeseed oil and olive oil are hard to beat.

You can even use oil for baking biscuits, cakes and bread. Some recipes that call for hard fat work perfectly well if you use oil instead. The general rule is to replace 100 grams (4 oz) of butter or margarine with 75 ml (five tablespoons) of oil. Although it is possible to use oil for pastry and crumble, I prefer reduced-fat spread.

It sounds a bit strange, I know, but in some cakes and puddings you can completely replace the fat with the same weight of prune purée. This works brilliantly in fruit cake (see recipe pages 188–9).

Top Tip: When making cakes and puddings, you can replace the fat with the same weight of prune purée.

4. Vitamins and Minerals

Zoe, aged seven, was an only child. Her mum, Judy, was a single parent and wasn't well off but had always done her best to make sure Zoe lacked nothing. Naturally enough, when Zoe saw school friends with a new toy or a new pair of shoes, she wanted the same. Judy tried not to disappoint her.

And when it came to food, she tried to give Zoe just what she wanted as well. The trouble was, Zoe didn't seem to want much these days.

'Zoe, for pudding, would you like an apple or some plums and custard?' asked Judy, clearing the plates from the table.

'Plums and custard,' muttered Zoe unenthusiastically, 'without the plums.'

Gradually Zoe had become more and more finicky – although she herself would deny this and point out that she was quite happy as long as she was given chicken Kiev, chips, custard and chocolate.

Judy served the bowl of steaming custard – with extra sugar just as Zoe liked it. She knew Zoe's diet wasn't ideal, but she comforted herself with the thought that she was giving her a double dose of a children's vitamin tablet every day.

Zoe had tried several brands of vitamin tablets. Usually, she would get no further than biting the head off a chewable animal shape before saying, 'Yuck! It makes me feel sick!' At last, after Judy had collected a row of bottles from which only one tablet had been taken, Zoe found a variety she liked. The bottle said 'one a day', but she was happy to take two.

The chosen brand wasn't cheap by any means, but Judy told herself she needn't worry about Zoe's diet – knowing that the double dose of vitamins would make up for any deficiencies.

Supplements, not substitutes

Sadly, vitamin tablets can never be a substitute for eating real food. They are not concentrated meal replacements.

To stay healthy, we need a regular supply of vitamins, minerals and trace elements. But the quantities we need are

minute. A balanced variety of foods that provides the protein, carbohydrate and fat we need will contain adequate quantities of vitamins and minerals. We cannot make ourselves extra healthy by taking more vitamins than our bodies can use. And an unbalanced diet like Zoe's is not corrected simply by taking extra vitamins.

Vitamins and minerals, together with some of the foods that contain them, are shown in Table 2. If you rely too much on highly processed foods – full of fat, sugar and modified starch – there is a risk that your child will fill up on calories without getting a proper balance of vitamins and minerals. If you follow the guidelines in this book and give a variety of more natural foods, vitamins and minerals will take care of themselves.

 Top Tip: *If your child has an unbalanced diet, you can't put it right with a vitamin tablet.*

Table 2

Vitamins and Minerals	
Vitamin/Mineral	**Food Sources**
Vitamin A (Retinol)	Liver, cod liver oil, fish, dairy products, fortified margarine, eggs (beta-carotene from carrots, apricots, green leafy vegetables, etc., is converted into vitamin A)
B Vitamins Thiamin (Vitamin B_1)	Wheat germ, whole wheat, wholemeal bread, nuts, pork, yeast extract, potatoes, peas, fortified breakfast cereals
Riboflavin (Vitamin B_2)	Liver, kidney, dairy products, yeast extract, wheat germ, beef, eggs, fortified cereals
Niacin (Nicotinic acid, Vitamin B_3)	Liver, kidney, meat, poultry, fish, yeast extract, peanuts, pulses, whole wheat, fortified breakfast cereals
Vitamin B_6 (Pyridoxine)	Vegetables, fish, meat, poultry, pulses, nuts, banana, avocado, breakfast cereals
Folate (Folacin, Folic acid)	Liver, whole grains, soya flour, blackeye beans, Brussels sprouts, broccoli, lettuce, pears, nuts, fortified cereals
Vitamin B_{12} (Cobalamin)	Liver, kidney, meat, poultry, fish, eggs, dairy products

Vitamin C (Ascorbic acid)	Fruits and vegetables e.g.: blackcurrants, guavas, oranges, lemons, strawberries, peppers, cauliflower, broccoli, potatoes
Vitamin D (Calciferol, Vitamins D_2 and and D_3)	Cod liver oil, oily fish, dairy products, infant formula, fortified margarine, eggs, liver, breakfast cereals
Vitamin E	Vegetable oils, nuts and seeds, margarines, whole grains
Vitamin K	Broccoli, cabbage, lettuce, tomatoes, potatoes, soya beans, liver (also made by bacteria in the intestine)
Calcium	Dairy products, fish (with bones), nuts, tahini, tofu, fortified bread
Iron	Meat, liver, kidney, poultry, fish, dark green vegetables, beans, lentils, tofu, dried fruit, fortified cereals
Magnesium	Nuts, cereals, pulses, yeast extract, meat
Zinc	Meat, fish, shellfish, wholegrain cereals, seeds, nuts

A few vitamins and minerals deserve a special mention.

The ACE vitamins

Vitamins A, C and E are important 'antioxidants'. This means they protect us against attack by 'free radicals'. I'm not talking about political extremists here. Free radicals are nasty chemicals that form in our bodies; the damage they cause leads to all sorts of problems (such as failing eyesight) as we get older, as well as cancers and heart disease. Vitamin C also helps to fight infections and heal wounds.

Fruits and vegetables are good sources of antioxidants.

Vitamin B$_{12}$

Vitamin B$_{12}$ comes from animal foods (such as liver, fish, meat, eggs and milk). It's wise for vegans to take a supplement as no vegetable food contains vitamin B$_{12}$ unless it's contaminated, for example, with manure (and I wouldn't recommend that as a supplement). Some cereals and vegetable margarines are fortified with vitamin B$_{12}$.

Adults keep a store of vitamin B$_{12}$ in the liver, but babies can become deficient very quickly. It is essential for vegan mothers who are feeding their babies purely on breast milk to take a supplement. Vitamin B$_{12}$ has a vital role in the development of the nervous system. There have been cases where a mild deficiency of vitamin B$_{12}$ in a breastfeeding mother has caused serious brain damage in her baby. Vitamin B$_{12}$ is a very safe supplement and there is no risk of having too much.

Young vegan children should also have a supplement of vitamin B$_{12}$. If you're not a vegan, you will almost certainly be getting enough.

Folic acid (Folate)

Folic acid is also one of the B vitamins although it's fortunate enough to be called by its name rather than being given a number. As you probably know, as well as eating foods containing folate, a supplement of 0.4 mg folic acid daily is recommended as soon as you start trying for a baby – and for the first three months of pregnancy. This reduces the risk of having a baby with spina bifida.

Recent research on adults has suggested that going short of folic acid can increase your risk of developing heart disease. Good sources of folate include liver, fortified breakfast cereals, blackeye beans, Brussels sprouts, nuts and leafy green vegetables.

Vitamin D

Vitamin D works with calcium to form strong bones and teeth. It's the sunshine vitamin: we make our own vitamin D when the skin is exposed to sunlight (but there's no point in giving your child skin cancer just to get a booster dose of vitamin D).

Poor diet combined with lack of sunlight can result in vitamin D deficiency – causing rickets in children, who have growing bones, and osteomalacia in adults. In the UK, this is more common among Asians in northern cities.

Foods that supply vitamin D include: oily fish (such as sardines, pilchards, salmon, mackerel, herring and fresh tuna); fortified margarine; fortified milk; and eggs.

Calcium

A good supply of calcium is essential for the healthy development of bones and teeth. During pregnancy and while breastfeeding, a woman needs to take in extra calcium to pass on to her baby.

Milk is an excellent source of calcium, but it doesn't always have to be taken as a drink: the milk you use to make custard, pancakes or scones all helps. Don't forget that skimmed milk contains just as much calcium as whole milk. Many recipes can be improved by adding extra skimmed milk powder. Quark (skimmed milk soft cheese) is great for making savoury sauces. Of course, all dairy products such as cheese, fromage frais and yoghurt are rich in calcium.

 Top Tip: *Skimmed milk contains just as much protein and calcium as whole milk; it's ideal from the age of five.*

Avoid giving whole cows' milk as a drink to a baby under the age of one. Indeed it may be sensible, particularly when there is a family history of allergies such as asthma and eczema, to delay the use of dairy products in general until after one year.

Apart from dairy products, useful sources of calcium include: green leafy vegetables; tahini (sesame seed paste); tinned fish (such as sardines and pilchards); and tofu. If you live in a hard water area, you have a little bit of calcium on tap – which all helps – unless you've fitted a water softener, of course. (While we're on the subject, water softened by an ion exchange system contains high levels of sodium and must not be used to prepare feeds for a baby.)

Iron

Iron is needed to make healthy red blood cells – the cells that give blood its red colour and carry oxygen to all parts of the body. Lack of iron causes anaemia.

Even in the developed world, iron deficiency is common in infancy. Anaemia can interfere with concentration and mental development, so it's really important to make sure your child is not going short of iron. The iron in liver, meat and fish is more easily absorbed into the body than iron in plant foods. Absorption of iron is improved by vitamin C (e.g. from fruit or fruit juice). On the other hand, cows' milk, tea and bran all reduce iron absorption.

If your child looks pale (even after removal of face paint and chalk dust) it may be nothing to do with anaemia. A better guide is to pull down the lower eyelid and see whether the lining is a healthy pink colour. Where there is doubt, a blood test will resolve it.

Zinc

Zinc is what's known as a trace element – essential, but only required in minute amounts. Being short of zinc will spoil your taste (when eating, I mean, not when choosing wallpaper). Zinc deficiency also impairs appetite and growth; it can weaken the immune response to infections and delay the healing of wounds. One study found that women whose babies were small for dates (i.e. smaller than expected at that stage of pregnancy) had low zinc levels.

Vegetarians who are not eating an adequate variety of foods, and people who fill up on empty calories from highly processed foods, are more at risk of zinc deficiency. But there's no need to give your child galvanised nails for tea. There's plenty of zinc in shellfish, meat, nuts, sunflower seeds and wholegrain cereals.

Sodium

Sodium is one mineral your child will definitely not go short of. Common salt's chemical name is sodium chloride. The minute amount that babies need is supplied by breast or formula milk. Too much salt is very dangerous for babies as their developing kidneys can't cope with it. Salt must never be added to baby foods.

You may have seen in the news the tragic case of the baby who died of salt overload because the parents, out of simple ignorance, were feeding it with unsuitable processed foods which were not formulated for infants. (You needn't worry about falling into the same trap as long as you avoid giving your baby any processed foods that are not labelled as suitable for infants.) Unfortunately, many convenience foods contain large quantities of added salt. As your child's kidneys mature, they can cope with more salt, but that doesn't mean it's a good idea to add salt to food! Food, in its natural state, contains all the sodium you and your child need. The trouble is that food manufacturers add stacks of salt to processed foods – including those aimed at children.

 Top Tip: *Never feed your baby processed products unless formulated for infants, and don't add salt to your baby's food.*

Why does this matter? Our high salt diet is linked with high blood pressure. If the average salt consumption in the UK were cut by one-third, it would probably prevent more strokes and heart attacks than all the drugs being prescribed for blood pressure. We've got used to the fact that blood pressure goes up as we get older, but this doesn't happen in communities with very low salt intakes from childhood.

High salt diets may also contribute to other health problems such as asthma, osteoporosis (brittle bones), and stomach cancer.

If you are used to adding salt at the table, now is the time to remove the saltcellar. By all means replace it with a pepper mill. Gradually cut down salt added during cooking to allow the family to get used to less salty food; it takes about a month for the palate to adjust to a big change. Before long, you will find heavily salted food unpleasant. Make full use of pepper, herbs, garlic, lemon and alcohol. (It's OK to use alcoholic drinks to flavour dishes such as casseroles cooked for children: the alcohol evaporates during cooking.) Where you think a little salt makes all the difference, consider using LoSalt or Solo which contain much less sodium.

That will be a good start. Unfortunately, though, 80 per cent of the salt we eat comes from processed foods; it's been added to the food before we get it to the kitchen.

Even factory-made bread generally contains far too much salt. Any supermarket worth its salt has lower sodium alternatives. Look for reduced-sodium loaves. And why buy a can of sweetcorn with added salt and sugar when you can buy one without? The fewer processed convenience foods you use, the more control you'll have over your family's salt intake.

This is an important health issue for your child and the adults in your family – especially if there is a family history of high blood pressure. Sadly, there will always be those who take even this advice with a pinch of salt!

Potassium

By contrast with sodium, potassium helps to lower blood pressure. So it's important not to go short of potassium. Food processing very unhelpfully removes potassium from food. Don't worry. You don't have to go round checking labels for potassium: it's another vital ingredient in fresh fruit and vegetables.

Should I give my child a supplement?

We've seen that all the vitamins and minerals your child needs for healthy growth and development are contained in satisfactory quantities in food. But what if your child doesn't eat the food in satisfactory quantities?

There's more to food than vitamins and minerals, and an unbalanced diet like Zoe's (see page 31) won't be put right by a supplement. If you want to give your child a supplement in addition to the best balance of foods you can manage, that's fine. We give our two daughters, aged seven and ten, a children's multivitamin and mineral tablet each day.

In fact, the Department of Health recommends vitamin drops (containing vitamins A, C and D) for all children between the ages of one and five – as well as for pregnant women. These drops are available from health visitors in child health clinics. Formula feeds are fortified with vitamin D. Breastfed babies are better off starting the drops at six months (or at one month if the mother might have been short of vitamins during pregnancy).

If you are buying a supplement for an older child, choose one that supplies the recommended daily amount (RDA) of a wide range of vitamins and minerals; but don't exceed the dose, and don't give big doses of one particularly favoured vitamin.

Some people take massive doses of vitamin C. The RDA is 60 mg (in the EU and USA) but you will see tablets of 1000 mg on sale. Although the RDA is just the amount required to

41

prevent deficiency (and may not actually be the optimum dose) there is no evidence that these huge doses do any good and, indeed, they may do some harm.

> **Top Tip:** *Don't give your child big doses of one favoured vitamin.*

Our own children eat a reasonable variety of fruits and vegetables each day in addition to taking 60 mg of vitamin C in their vitamin tablet – so they're well covered. When people take more than 250 mg of vitamin C a day, the excess comes straight out in the urine. There must be millions of pounds' worth of vitamin C coursing through our sewers (but whether that improves the health of our rats, I have no idea).

A LOT OF VITAMIN C ENDS UP IN THE SEWERS

The Simple Secret of Success

How to Give Your Child a Balanced Diet

So food contains a mixture of protein, carbohydrate, fat, vitamins, minerals and, of course, water. Obviously you are keen to give your child the best balance of all these constituents to promote healthy growth and development and protection against future disease. But the big question is: how on earth do you keep track of all the nutrients your child is taking in to make sure the balance is right?

The Balancing Act

Most importantly, don't worry. You don't have to be a qualified dietitian to be a successful parent (although some people manage both). There's no need to weigh food portions, consult food composition tables or undertake a computer analysis of

43

your child's nutritional status. It's much simpler than that.

All you have to do is to understand that there are five food groups:

- cereals and starchy foods
- fruit and vegetables
- milk and dairy products
- meat and high-protein foods
- fatty and sugary foods.

And you only need to bother about the first four. If your child has a good variety of foods selected from each of the first four groups, everything else will take care of itself. The fifth group is foods containing lots of fat, lots of sugar or both. You don't really need any foods from this group; there's quite enough fat and carbohydrate in the first four. (If you give a lot of foods from group five, your child will be getting too many calories without enough nourishment.)

The point is that no single food contains everything you and your child need. What's lacking in a food from one group will be supplied by foods from the other groups. Every day, try to choose foods from *each* of the four important groups. Aim to use a *variety* of foods from each group. This is essential because foods all have different levels of vital nutrients. For instance, pears are excellent and I hope your child likes them. But if you serve raw pear every day – and nothing else from the fruit and vegetable group – your child will become deficient in vitamin C.

 Top Tip: *Every day, give your child a variety of foods from each of the four important food groups.*

Table 3 shows common foods in their groups. Although the list doesn't include every available food, it should help you to place others where they belong.

Table 3

The Five Food Groups

1. Cereals and Starchy Foods
★ Bread, including wholemeal, mixed grain, granary loaves, rye bread, white bread, French bread, pitta bread, rolls, baps
★ Crumpets, crispbreads, matzos, breadsticks, rice cakes
★ Breakfast cereals, muesli
★ Oats (including porridge), barley, rye, wheat, bulgar wheat, buckwheat, millet, maize, polenta, semolina, couscous, tapioca
★ Rice, including brown rice, wild rice, baby rice
★ Pasta: spaghetti, lasagna, tagliatelle, macaroni, noodles, etc.
★ Potatoes, sweet potato, cassava, yam, tavo

2. Fruit and Vegetables
★ Salad vegetables, including lettuce, cucumber, tomatoes, peppers, etc.
★ All vegetables (not potatoes) – fresh, frozen or canned
★ All fruit – fresh, frozen or canned
★ Dried fruit, e.g. prunes, figs, apricots, raisins, sultanas
★ Fruit juice

3. Milk and Dairy Products
★ Milk – whole, semi-skimmed or skimmed
★ Cheese, e.g. Cheddar, cottage cheese, quark, Parmesan, pecorino
★ Yoghurt
★ Fromage frais
★ Buttermilk

---

4. Meat and High-Protein Foods
★ Meat: beef, pork, lamb, bacon, ham, rabbit, venison
★ Meat products: sausages, burgers
★ Poultry: chicken, turkey
★ White fish – cod, haddock, coley, plaice, sole, etc.
★ Oily fish – mackerel, herring, pilchards, sardines, salmon
★ Shellfish – scallops, oysters, cockles, etc.
★ Nuts: hazelnuts, almonds, walnuts, peanuts
★ Seeds: sunflower, sesame, pumpkin, flaxseeds/linseeds
★ Eggs
★ Pulses: lentils, chickpeas, beans (e.g. baked beans, kidney beans, broad beans, blackeye beans, soya beans), peas, split peas
★ Dahl, hummus, tofu, textured vegetable protein (TVP)
★ Quorn

5. Fatty/Sugary Foods
Fatty foods (some also have high sugar content):
★ Fat spreads, margarine, butter
★ Olive oil, rapeseed oil, corn oil, sunflower oil, safflower oil, soya oil, sesame seed oil, grapeseed oil, walnut oil, groundnut (peanut) oil, palm oil, coconut oil, 'vegetable oil'
★ Suet, lard, dripping
★ Oil-based dressings, fatty sauces, mayonnaise
★ Cream, ice cream
★ Cakes, biscuits, puddings, pastries, crisps
★ Chocolate, chocolate spread, toffee/butterscotch sauces
★ Coconut bars

Sugary foods (some also have high fat content):
★ Sweets
★ Sweet snacks
★ Sweetened drinks, squashes
★ Sugar, jams

Balancing for Bigger People

As an adult, the bulk of your food should come from the first two groups – the starchy foods and the fruit and vegetable group. Choose plenty of wholegrain cereal foods from porridge to pasta. Have at least five portions of fruit and vegetables a day; this could be two pieces of fruit and three servings of vegetables. Three servings from the dairy group will give you essential calcium; skimmed milk taken in tea throughout the day, a low-fat yoghurt, and quark added to a pasta dish would each count as one serving. Two different servings from the high-protein group (such as a piece of fish and a portion of beans) will give you all the protein you need for the day.

Figure 1 ('Balance of Good Health') shows this balanced adult diet on a plate. See how much of the plate is taken up by fruit and vegetables and by cereals and starchy foods – and how little is taken up by meat and dairy products.

By the time your child is five, this grown-up balance is ideal. Whenever possible, adults and children should sit at the same table and share the same food.

Ten Tasty Snacks for Toddlers

Before you reach for the crisps and biscuits, try some of these:

1. a bowl of cereal with sliced banana and milk
2. natural yoghurt with added fruit
3. tinned sardines mashed onto toast and cut into fingers
4. rice cakes with cottage cheese
5. pieces of cold chicken with fruit (e.g. peach slices)
6. raw vegetables (e.g. sugarsnap peas, sticks of carrot or pepper)
7. mini-sandwiches (e.g. wholemeal bread and ham or peanut butter)
8. home-made flapjack, carrot cake or banana cake
9. malt bread or fruit scone
10. breadsticks with a glass of milk.

Figure 1

The Balance of Good Health

Fruit and vegetables

Bread, other cereals and potatoes

BREAKFAST Cereal

Meat, fish and alternatives

Foods containing fat
Foods and drinks containing sugar

Milk and dairy foods

There are five main groups of valuable foods

Balancing for Beginners

Don't try to impose adult standards on your toddler who is already making the difficult journey from infancy to independence. Babies need to get half their calories from fat and, to start with, they rely on breast or formula milk. It takes a few years to adapt to an adult way of eating. Here are ten top tips for toddlers:

1. Don't overdo the wholegrain cereals. A toddler's tummy can be quickly filled with high-fibre, wholegrain foods

DON'T FILL YOUR TODDLER UP WITH FIBRE

(such as brown rice and wholemeal bread) leaving too little room for other important foods.

2. Don't strive to give your toddler a grown-up balance of the four important food groups as shown in Figure 1 ('Balance of Good Health').

3. Do choose some foods from each of the four main food groups every day and offer as much variety as possible.

4. Four times a day, give your toddler something from the fruit and vegetable group (such as pineapple pieces on pizza, or sugarsnap peas as a snack).

5. Every day, put a portion of meat, liver, poultry or fish on the menu as these are good sources of iron. If your toddler is vegetarian, fruit or fruit juice will increase the absorption of iron from plant foods (such as tofu, beans, lentils, greens, bread and fortified cereals).

6. Don't give your child low-fat dairy products such as skimmed milk and low-fat yoghurt before five years. If your toddler is eating and growing well, you can introduce semi-skimmed milk from two years.

7. Give your toddler three-quarters of a pint of milk a day (this can include breast milk). Don't forget that the milk on cereal and in cooking all counts. (Drinking too much milk between meals can spoil a toddler's appetite at mealtimes.) Unsweetened soya drink with added calcium is an alternative for vegan toddlers.
8. Offer plenty of water to drink.
9. Don't get your child hooked on flavoured drinks: fizzy drinks, fruit squashes and juices can all attack the teeth.
10. Don't give your toddler tea to drink. Ever popular with chimpanzees, tea is not a good drink for young children as it reduces the absorption of iron from food. The same goes for coffee.

 Top Tip: Give your toddler plenty of high-energy foods; adult guidelines for healthy eating apply from five years of age.

Success on a Plate

So, remember the four main food groups. Choose a variety of foods from each group every day and you won't go wrong. Of course, your child won't eat everything you put on the plate (see pages 91–2). And children must be allowed to dislike some foods. So if rice is a definite reject, just use other foods from the same group instead (such as pasta, bread, yam or potato). You don't have to name the nutrients, monitor the minerals or count the calories: the food groups take care of it for you.

'My Child's Not a Carnivore!'

Feeding Your Vegetarian or Vegan Child

You don't need meat (animal flesh) to stay healthy (unless you're the animal it belongs to) and more and more people are following the cows' example and adopting a vegetarian way of life. Indeed, eating a plant-based diet may give you a health advantage: on average, vegetarians have lower cholesterol levels and are less likely to suffer from obesity, heart disease and certain cancers. But you don't have to stop eating meat to enjoy all these health benefits.

Of course, if you copy the cow too closely and adopt a restricted vegetarian diet, you will soon run into nutritional problems. And when you bring a child up as a vegetarian, you need to take extra care to avoid deficiency of any vital nutrients. The more foods that are excluded from the diet, the greater the risk of deficiency.

A VEGETARIAN DIET MAY HAVE HEALTH ADVANTAGES

What Sort of Vegetarian?

The most popular form of vegetarian diet is *lacto-ovo-vegetarian* – animal flesh is excluded but milk and eggs are allowed. If you are a *lacto-vegetarian*, you cut out eggs as well. A *vegan* diet excludes all foods of animal origin – meat, milk, eggs, honey and additives derived from animals (such as whey, lecithin, gelatine and vitamin D_3). Vegan babies are allowed human breast milk, but strict vegans would want to avoid brands of soya formula containing vitamin D from lanolin (which comes from the wool of living sheep).

Table 4 should make things clearer. It shows you the sources of protein in the various types of vegetarian diet and which nutrients might be in short supply.

You can see there is more risk of nutritional deficiencies on a vegan diet than on a vegetarian diet that allows dairy products

Table 4

Type of diet	Foods excluded	Sources of protein	Nutrients that may be in short supply
Lacto-ovo-vegetarian	Red meat Offal Poultry Fish	Milk Cheese Yoghurt Eggs Beans Lentils Soya Products Nuts and Seeds Quorn	Energy (calories) Iron
Lacto-vegetarian	Red Meat Offal Poultry Fish Eggs	Milk Cheese Yoghurt Beans Lentils Soya Products Nuts and Seeds Quorn	Energy (calories) Iron Vitamin D
Vegan	Red meat Offal Poultry Fish Eggs Milk Cheese Yoghurt	Beans Lentils Soya Products Nuts and Seeds Quorn	Energy (calories) Iron Vitamin A and D Protein Vitamin B_2 (Riboflavin) Vitamin B_{12} Calcium Zinc

and eggs. Table 5 shows where to obtain the nutrients that your child is most likely to be lacking on a vegan diet.

Table 5

What your vegan child could be lacking	Where to get it
Energy	Vegetable oils (add to starchy foods such as rice) Smooth nut or seed butters*
Iron	(Fruit or fruit juice increases iron absorption) Fortified breakfast cereals Dark green vegetables Bread Beans and lentils Tofu Dried fruit Curry powder (mild!) Molasses
Vitamin A/Beta-carotene	Tomatoes Carrots Peppers Apricots Vitamin drops
Vitamin D	Fortified breakfast cereals Fortified soya milk, cheeses and yoghurts Fortified margarine Sunshine (half an hour a day is enough) Vitamin drops
Protein	Beans, lentils Soya products (e.g. tofu, soya milk)

	Smooth nut or seed butters* Quorn
Vitamin B$_2$ (Riboflavin)	Wheat germ Finely ground almonds* Soya beans Fortified soya milk Green leafy vegetables Avocados Carob flour
Vitamin B$_{12}$	Fortified breakfast cereals Fortified soya milk Tofu, fortified textured soya protein Quorn Vitamin supplements
Calcium	Fortified soya drinks Soya mince, soya cheese Tofu and tempeh Tahini paste* Bread (especially white) Finely ground almonds* Molasses
Zinc	Wheat germ Cashews, peanuts, walnuts, almonds* Sunflower, sesame, pumpkin seeds* Soya cheese, soya flour Lentils, chickpeas, split peas Grape-nuts Wholemeal bread

*Don't give nuts or seeds until your child is *at least* six months. Extra care is needed if you have allergies in your family: avoid peanuts (and products such as peanut butter and unrefined groundnut oil) for the first three years. Whole nuts should not be given to children under five because of the risk of choking.

55

Top Tip: *If you are a vegan and breastfeeding, it is essential to protect your child from vitamin B$_{12}$ deficiency.*

Here are ten tips to help you raise a healthy, perhaps even beefy, vegetarian child:

1. If you are a vegan, continue breastfeeding for the first year, if you can, but take a vitamin supplement containing B$_{12}$; your child may need one too.
2. Use soya-based infant formula until your child is two years old to provide essential protein. Unlike cows' milk, soya-based infant formula contains added sugar so follow the directions on the product to avoid tooth decay.
3. Infant formula contains added iron. If your baby is having breast milk (and no infant formula) beyond six months, give an iron supplement.
4. From six months, introduce plenty of iron-rich foods (see Table 2 on pages 33–4) and give fruit (or fruit juice) at the same time to increase iron absorption.
5. Following the guidelines in 'Starting Solids' (page 63), use as wide a variety of foods as possible to provide essential nutrients listed in Table 5.
6. Avoid filling your child up with high-fibre foods (e.g. wholemeal bread, high-bran breakfast cereals) and watery foods (e.g. dilute porridge, some fruits) or the diet may be short on energy (calories). Include high-energy fruits such as banana and avocado.
7. Add vegetable oil to baby cereals to increase energy

content. A teaspoon of oil is easy to mix with food (or drinks) and provides essential fatty acids.

8. If you are a vegan, choose olive oil, rapeseed oil or soya oil rather than sunflower, safflower or corn oil to keep up the level of omega-3 fatty acids.

9. Use pulses (peas, beans, lentils) with grains (e.g. rice, bread, pasta) to avoid any protein deficiency caused by missing amino acids. Try to include two different sources of protein at each meal.

10. Give vitamin drops containing vitamins A, C and D (available from your health visitor) from six months to five years – unless you are giving a multivitamin to include the B vitamins as well. Half an hour of sunshine a day, with just hands and face exposed, will top up your child's vitamin D (but if you live in the UK, you probably think that's pretty useless information).

 Top Tip: *Giving your child a combination of pulses and grains will supply quality protein.*

'Which End Does It Go?'

Practical Tips on Feeding Your Baby

'Do you want to breastfeed your baby?' I asked Sandra in the antenatal clinic.

'Oh no,' she replied. 'It doesn't seem natural somehow. Makes me feel funny to think about it. And it's not very

SOME PARENTS
DON'T SEE BREAST FEEDING
AS NATURAL...

I KNOW, BUT THEY'VE BOOBED.

59

hygienic, is it? I couldn't be doing with all that. Think of the inconvenience if you need to give a feed when you're out!'

Sandra had made up her mind, and I wasn't likely to change it. However, she couldn't have been more wrong when she suggested breastfeeding wasn't natural. And what could be more convenient than having an automatic supply of milk at just the right temperature – and no bottles to sterilise?

Top Tip: *Breastfeeding is more convenient than sterilising bottles.*

Are There Any Other Advantages to Breastfeeding?

Yes. Here are some of them:

- Breast milk contains special ingredients that protect against infection; bottle-fed babies suffer more infections, especially gastroenteritis (diarrhoea and vomiting).
- Unlike powdered milk, which can be made up incorrectly, breast milk is always produced at the right concentration.
- Breastfeeding in the first six months, especially in families with a history of asthma or eczema, can help to protect the baby against allergies.
- Breastfeeding is good for mothers too: it helps the womb to return to normal size, and uses up excess fat stored during pregnancy.
- Breastfeeding is cheaper than bottle feeding. The infant formula, bottles, teats and sterilising equipment cost a lot

more than the little bit of extra nourishment required by a
breastfeeding mother.
- The physical closeness of breastfeeding is very comforting
  and helps the emotional bonding between mother and baby.

Mind you, a disadvantage of breastfeeding is that it excludes
dad. I know from personal experience: no matter how much a
father longs to get up at night and breastfeed the baby, that
privilege belongs exclusively to the mother. Heather was always
very understanding about this and let me change more nappies
by way of compensation. Of course, mum could always take
the trouble to express milk so that dad can give night feeds,
once the milk supply is well established.

I'm Worried that I Won't Have Enough Breast Milk

The secret of establishing a good milk supply is to understand
that it depends on the demand. Whenever breastfed babies are
given unnecessary drinks of boiled water, or juice, or formula
milk, the breasts go unstimulated and milk supply starts to
decline.

Even if you don't think that you will continue to breastfeed,
it's still worth starting; any breastfeeding you can do will help
your baby. It's ideal to put your baby to the breast immediately
after birth – as long as there's no doubt about breathing. (A
crying baby is breathing.)

Some babies latch on immediately; others take longer to
learn. So stick with it. Getting over the early difficulties with
breastfeeding is more than half the battle. Your midwife will
help you get started and your health visitor will be able to

advise you after that. The National Childbirth Trust can be a great support as well.

Bottling Out

Breastfeeding isn't for everyone. Some women, like Sandra, just don't want to do it. Others desperately want to but, despite really trying, can't manage it. You might feel you have to switch to bottle feeding if you're going back to work.

 Whatever it is that drives you to the bottle, it's good to know that your baby can thrive and flourish on modern infant formula – so there's nothing to feel guilty about. Unlike ordinary cows' milk which is quite unsuitable for babies under one year, infant formula has been modified to make it similar to breast milk.

Which formula?

There is a wide choice of infant formula milks, but they can be divided into two main groups according to the type of protein in them – 'whey dominant' and 'casein dominant'. Don't worry. It's not at all complicated. You remember Little Miss Muffett who sat on her tuffet, eating her curds and whey? When milk curdles, the lumpy bits (or milk curds) are made of a protein called casein. The watery part that separates from the curds is called whey.

Whey dominant formulas have more whey than casein (in a ratio of about 60:40) like human breast milk. Whey protein is easier for small babies to digest and these formulas are a good choice for babies under three months.

Casein dominant formulas have less whey than casein (about 20:80) like cows' milk. These are marketed as suitable for the more hungry baby – the idea being that the casein takes longer to digest. In fact, though, there' s no reason why you shouldn't use a whey-based formula until switching to cows' milk at one year.

Follow-on formulas may be given to bottle-fed or breastfed babies from six months. These are modified cows' milk with added iron and vitamin D.

Soya formulas are available for babies who are allergic to cows' milk protein or cannot tolerate lactose (milk sugar). As a general rule, they should only be used on medical advice.

If you have any doubts about the right formula for your baby, have a chat with your health visitor.

Starting Solids

When to start
Breast milk or infant formula will meet all your baby's nutritional needs for the first four to six months of life. It's not good for babies to start solids too soon. On the other hand, if your baby throws away the bottle and snatches your pork chop, you've probably left it too late. So what are the clues that a baby is ready for weaning? (Funny word that. Try saying it ten times if you don't believe me.) Try starting solids when your baby:

- is four to six months old
- still seems hungry after a good milk feed
- goes back to waking for a night feed after sleeping through

63

LOOK OUT FOR CLUES THAT YOUR BABY IS READY FOR WEANING

- starts wanting to be fed more frequently
- shows an interest in your food.

Top Tip: Breast or formula milk is all your baby needs for the first four months; start solids by six months.

Even if your baby cries a lot, it's better not to start solids earlier than four months. Babies cry for various reasons, and weaning too early could raise the risk of obesity and future heart disease. Giving nothing but breast milk for the first six months may reduce the risk of developing allergies, especially when there is a family history of conditions such as asthma and eczema. We

64

set out to do this with our first daughter, Serena, but at four months she made her feelings clear and we started solids (although Heather continued to breastfeed for over a year). After four months, be guided by your baby. But after six months, milk alone is not enough and the introduction of solids should not be left any later than this.

What to start with

Jenny was excited but a little anxious. Her first baby, Matthew, was now four months old and seemed ready to start solids. But what should she give him? She was worried that he might be allergic to something, and she'd heard that you could overload a baby's kidneys by giving the wrong foods. Her mother would have told her what to do, but she'd gone back to Australia and Jenny didn't feel she could be on the phone every five minutes asking for advice.

So she found it really reassuring to go to the supermarket and see so many little jars of food clearly labelled as suitable for babies of Matthew's age. She picked up a jar of vegetable purée and was pleased to see that no salt or artificial flavours, colours or preservatives had been added.

Jenny confidently put a few jars in her trolley. It was so good to know that these foods had been specially selected and prepared for babies. 'How did people cope before these convenient baby foods were available?' she wondered.

The answer, of course, is that they gave their babies ordinary, simple, unprocessed food such as puréed vegetables and fruit. I strongly recommend that you do the same!

Getting Off to a Solid Start

Ten tips for stress-free introduction of solids

1. Choose a time when you and your baby are relaxed. Lunchtime is usually a good choice. Give at least half the normal milk feed first or your baby is likely to get frustrated and angry.
2. Start with a teaspoon of vegetable or fruit purée or baby rice with milk. A plastic weaning spoon is ideal. Equipment does not have to be sterilised but should be carefully washed in clean, hot water.
3. Food can be served at room temperature or warm (not hot). After warming food, always stir thoroughly and test the temperature on your wrist.
4. One teaspoonful during the lunchtime feed is enough to begin with. Remember to give the rest of the milk! At this stage, your baby is just learning about taste and texture. Milk is still the main source of nourishment.
5. Introduce one new food at a time and give it for two or three days to make sure there are no unwanted effects.
6. Gradually increase the amount and the thickness of purées.
7. Don't push the spoon in too far or your baby will gag.
8. Don't worry if the food comes squelching back out. This is normal. Your baby will soon start sucking food from the spoon.
9. Don't leave your baby alone with food. Never add solids, such as rusks, to drinks as it can cause choking.
10. Above all, relax. If your baby doesn't seem to want the food, simply try again another day. There's plenty of time.

Isn't it safer to give properly formulated baby foods?

Jenny is not alone. A lot of first-time parents are feeling their way without the guidance of the extended family. The food industry feeds their impression that babies need special foods prepared by experts. Those reassuring labels can be misleading.

Of course there's 'no added salt' in a baby food. And there will be 'no artificial colours or preservatives' as these are banned substances. But a recent survey by the Consumers' Association found that 40 per cent of baby foods had added sugar or fruit juice, and 40 per cent contained added starch. The modified starch in processed foods adds bulk and calories without nourishment.

No doubt you can thrive on the contents of those little jars – especially if you're a food manufacturer as it's a multi-million-pound industry. But your baby may be better off with food you've prepared yourself.

The sensible way to use these ready-made baby meals is as an occasional convenience, for example when you're going out and haven't had time to prepare anything. When buying a baby food, always check it is recommended for your baby's age. If your baby is under six months, avoid products containing egg and gluten (wheat protein). Make sure the food hasn't passed its 'Sell by' date and that the seal on the container hasn't been broken.

Top Tip: *You are the best person to prepare food for your baby.*

Nobody does it better

So you are the best person to prepare your baby's first non-milk foods. Although many parents pale at the thought of preparing their baby's food themselves, the truth is that you don't need the skills or kitchen of a gourmet chef to produce first-class results. All you need is a little information and a few things you would find in any normal kitchen – such as a fork

Table 6

Allergy Alert

People can be allergic to all sorts of things, but some foods are more likely than others to provoke allergy or other unwanted reactions in a baby. Avoid these foods until your baby is at least six months old:

★ Wheat and other foods containing gluten
★ Eggs
★ Nuts and seeds (and spreads such as peanut butter and tahini)
★ Fish and shellfish
★ Citrus fruits (e.g. oranges) and their juices
★ Cows' milk and follow-on milk
★ Milk products (e.g. yoghurt, fromage frais, cheese)

Extra care is needed if you have asthma, eczema, hay fever or other allergies in your family. It may be wise to avoid particular foods for longer than six months; this is something to discuss with your health visitor or doctor. When foods are excluded, it's vital to make sure that your baby's diet is balanced. Your doctor may suggest referring you to a dietitian.

Nuts – especially peanuts – and certain seeds cause serious allergic reactions in some people. If you have allergies in your family, don't give your child peanuts (or products such as peanut butter and groundnut oil) for the first three years. That means checking food labels.

In any case, whole nuts should not be given to children under five years because of the risk of choking.

---

for mashing and a sieve to produce purées (and a bit of food, of course).

Here are some examples of suitable first solids:

- cooked, puréed vegetables such as carrot, potato, yam, parsnip, cauliflower, courgette or leek with **no added salt**
- raw, puréed banana, avocado, mango or soft ripe pear
- stewed fruit such as apple, apricot, peach or pear with no added sugar
- gluten-free cereals (e.g. baby rice, sago, cornmeal, millet) mixed to a smooth paste with breast milk or formula.

It will come as a bit of a shock to your baby that food doesn't have to be liquid and taste of milk. To begin with, purées should be quite sloppy – like thick soup.

When convenient, purée larger quantities of cooked food and freeze some (e.g. in ice cube trays). A small hand-held blender makes light work of remaining lumps – and is delightfully easy to clean.

What Next?

Over the next few weeks, gradually increase the amount of food you give your baby. Four weeks after starting solids, you might be giving a couple of teaspoons at breakfast and two or three teaspoons at lunchtime. Start giving solids first and finishing off with milk. Eight weeks after that first teaspoon of purée, your baby could be having two or more *tablespoons* of solids (but still given on a plastic teaspoon, of course) at three meals a day, followed by breast milk or formula. Be guided by your baby's appetite – not by what your friends are giving their babies.

In addition to those three meals of purée topped up with breast milk or formula, give a milk feed in the morning and one at bedtime. Regular breastfeeding, or about 600 ml (1 pint)

of formula a day, will supply your baby with calcium and other vital nutrients. Don't give ordinary cows' milk as a drink until your baby is a year old, but you can mix some with food or use it in cooking from six months. If you have allergies in your family, it's wise to avoid general dairy products such as cows' milk, full-fat yoghurt, fromage frais and cheese until your baby is eight to twelve months old.

From Six to Nine Months

Keep up the breastfeeding or 600 ml (1 pint) of formula a day. Babies can become very attached to their bottles and this is a good time to start using a feeding cup for some milk feeds and for water. After all, you don't want your child struggling to boot the bottle before university.

Try to bring in a wide variety of foods now. There might be several different foods mixed together on one spoon, for example in a lasagne, but it's still wise to introduce one *new* food at a time. This is an important time of discovery. You are laying the foundation for your child's future appreciation of food. Meeting lots of new smells, tastes and textures now can make life a lot easier in the toddler years.

> **Top Tip:** Give your baby lots of different foods between six and nine months, but introduce one new food at a time.

Have your baby's highchair at the family table and eat together whenever you can. Food should now be mashed or minced, not puréed, and your baby can share the family meal – unless you're having chicken Vindaloo or something else a bit too educational. Learning to season without salt is good for the whole family, but if you do use salt in your cooking, remove food for your baby before it's seasoned.

Lumpier food takes a little getting used to after purées, and your baby may look disgusted at first. Don't worry. That phase will soon pass. From six months onwards you can also give 'finger foods' (which are foods picked up in the fingers, not necessarily foods made of fingers – although 'toast fingers' are a popular choice). Here are a few suggestions for first finger foods:

- toast fingers
- breadsticks
- rusks
- pieces of pitta bread or chapatti
- soft, cooked vegetables, e.g. cauliflower, peas, carrot
- pieces of peeled, soft, ripe pear or peach
- chunks of banana.

First finger foods should be soft (or, like rusks and bread, should soften quickly in the mouth). Once your child is chomping cheerfully, you can add harder finger foods such as pieces of red or green pepper, carrot sticks, peeled apple and lumps of Cheddar cheese.

Giving finger foods will encourage your baby to chew. There's no need to wait for teeth to appear. At this age, babies investigate their world by transferring as much of it as they can to the mouth. So, given the chance, your baby will grab food and discover that it's good to eat. Stay nearby to guard against choking. Finger food is great fun, but you won't think so when it's trodden into the carpet. Position the highchair on a washable floor or protective covering, further away from that freshly-papered wall than your baby is able to throw.

From Nine to Twelve Months

Your baby will enjoy holding a spoon and, with practice, will gradually get more of the food where it's meant to go. Meanwhile, you can prevent malnutrition with another spoon.

Whether your family is just you and your baby, or enough people to fill a dining hall, eating together is most important.

You can't build good relationships without paying some attention to each other. Mealtimes provide a natural opportunity for this – an opportunity which is lost if all faces are fixed on the TV screen. As well as learning to appreciate good food, families that regularly share meals together are more likely to appreciate one another than those that don't.

It's ideal for your baby to share in three family meals a day at this stage and eat the same food as everyone else, although some of it will need to be chopped into small pieces or minced.

Don't add salt to your baby's food. If you use processed foods, like baked beans, choose brands with less added salt. Avoid heavily salted products such as anchovies.

Adding sugar to food adds calories without nourishment; it also attacks the teeth and encourages a sweet tooth, which is asking for trouble in the future. If necessary, you can sweeten your baby's food with dried fruit, mashed banana, or milk (breast or formula). Honey is just another form of sugar; it should not be given to babies under a year old as it can cause a serious illness called infant botulism.

Remember the four important food groups (page 7). All members of the family, including your baby, should eat a variety

of foods from each group every day. By joining in family meals from the outset, your child can meet an interesting diversity of foods. Children who are fed separately from adults, on nothing but children's convenience meals, are not learning to enjoy a wide range of different foods (and they may grow up thinking fish are naturally rectangular).

Top Tip: *Your baby will learn a lot from joining in family meals and watching you enjoy your food.*

In between the three main meals, your baby will need snacks such as chopped fruit or vegetables. Carry on breastfeeding or give about 600 ml (1 pint) of formula a day.

From One Year Onwards

By the age of one year, children should be sharing meals with the rest of the family and at least attempting to feed themselves. Let your child use fingers or a spoon – but not a sharp knife, of course. It's also wise to use plates and bowls that bounce. A bit of mess now, while your child has fun with food and becomes better at putting it in the right place, could save a lot of trouble later on. Spoon-feeding may seem efficient but it's not very educational. On the other hand, children learn a lot by watching the rest of the family enjoying meals together.

Make sure your child has at least half a pint of milk a day – either as a drink or mixed with food – to supply calcium to growing bones and teeth. This could be breast milk or formula but, from the age of one, whole cows' milk may be given as a drink. Other dairy foods, such as yoghurt, cheese and fromage frais, are additional sources of calcium. If your child is allergic to cows' milk, give unsweetened soya drink fortified with calcium. Don't use low-fat products for children under five, although, as I said earlier, semi-skimmed milk can be started from two years.

Eating together as a family should ensure that you offer your child something from each of the four main food groups at most meals. Snacks such as mini-sandwiches or pieces of vegetable or fruit, will keep your toddler going between meals. Try to avoid highly processed snacks such as crisps and bought biscuits. (I'm not suggesting that you should steal biscuits, but if you make your own, they needn't be full of unwanted ingredients such as hydrogenated vegetable oil.)

'What Should I Give My Child to Drink?'

Milk and water are the best drinks.

Milk (breast or formula) is all a baby needs to begin with and milk continues to be an important source of nutrients (especially calcium) when your child is eating well. Whole cows' milk can be given as a drink from one year; if your child is eating and growing well, you can start semi-skimmed milk at two years and skimmed milk at five; give at least half a pint a day. Unsweetened soya drink fortified with calcium is an alternative for vegan children or those allergic to cows' milk. Remember that soya-based infant formula contains added sugar; prolonged contact with the teeth can lead to tooth decay.

75

Water is the only other drink your child really needs. It's safe and it's satisfying to children who haven't been brought up on sweet drinks. All drinks that contain sugar (including natural fruit juices with no *added* sugar) can be harmful to the teeth. If you do give your child flavoured drinks, keep to unsweetened natural fruit juices (diluted) and serve them with meals – not in between. 'Sparkling' (fizzy) water isn't very kind to teeth either, so don't give it as a regular drink.

Some young children become so hooked on squash, and drink so much of it, that they don't absorb their food properly and have a poor appetite; this results in malnutrition, stunted growth, anaemia, diarrhoea and irritability. Apart from that, they're fine.

Get your child off the bottle as soon as you can. The slow delivery of drinks through a teat is bad for teeth – and you can't learn to speak if you've always got a bottle stuck in your mouth. A beaker with a lid is an improvement; a cup is better still.

Low-sugar and 'diet' drinks contain artificial sweeteners and I certainly wouldn't want to give my children big doses of those – especially saccharin.

If your child is already a juice junkie, gradually make the drinks weaker and weaker until you're giving slightly tinted water.

Tea and coffee are *not* suitable for under-fives: they block the absorption of iron from food.

'That's Your Second Packet Today!'

Getting It Right with Sweets and Treats

Have you ever seen the dramatic calming effect that a bar of chocolate or a bag of crisps can have on a screaming toddler in a supermarket? It can be almost miraculous. Surely anything that has that effect has earned its place in the parents' essential survival kit. (Mind you, I could produce a similar result with a quick injection of Valium, but I don't think parents should carry that around with them.)

The problem with using a quick fix of sweets or crisps to calm a screaming child is that it teaches the child to behave badly – to repeat the behaviour that was rewarded. This is tricky because, as a harassed parent, you know that hunger makes your child irritable so, before you set out on that shopping trip, you pack a snack. And sweets, chocolate, biscuits and crisps come in such convenient packs.

 Top Tip: *Calming a screaming child with sweets or crisps trains the child to scream.*

Good or Bad?

Of course, even if you were to calm your screaming child with a salmon and salad sandwich, you would still be rewarding bad behaviour. Whatever food you choose, there are good and bad times to give it. But are there good and bad foods? Is there really anything wrong with sweets, biscuits and crisps, or are they actually good top-up fuels for energetic kids?

One problem with sweets, and other foods packed with *sugar*, is that they cause tooth decay. You might think this doesn't matter if fluoride has been added to the water supply and you brush the teeth thoroughly. Fluoride is a help and brushing carefully twice a day is essential, but teeth can still be damaged by frequent contact with sugary foods and drinks.

Another problem is that sugar in these products fills children with calories rather than nourishment. In the end, by eating too many foods that are full of energy but lacking nutrients, you could become overweight and undernourished.

As well as sugar, manufactured snack foods such as chocolate, cakes and biscuits contain a lot of *fat*. It's important that toddlers are not deprived of fat, but these products often contain large quantities of unfriendly saturated and trans fats that nobody needs at all. So read the labels (see table on page 23) and remember that 'hydrogenated vegetable oil' is something to avoid as much as possible. If you can find the time to bake your own cakes and biscuits (see recipes pages 187–9), the fat content will be under your control. Once children reach the age of five, of course, they should be eating a lower fat diet as recommended for adults.

The discovery that chocolate contains antioxidants (those wonderful substances that mop up nasty chemicals called 'free radicals') has led to some wild claims in the press. Advice to 'eat chocolate to help your heart' overlooks the fact that any benefit from the antioxidants in chocolate will probably be outweighed by the effects of the saturated fat you get with it.

"I READ THAT CHOCOLATE'S GOOD FOR THE HEART!"

Fat comes with lots of *salt* in crisps and similar savoury snacks. In the West, blood pressure typically rises as we get older and this contributes to our high rates of stroke and heart disease. We can put a lot of this down to the large amounts of salt in Western diets. Excessive salt intake may play a part in other health problems too (see pages 39–40).

The thing about salt is that if you eat a lot of it, food doesn't taste right without it. If you give your child a lot of salty snacks like crisps, you can expect complaints when you make soup without salt.

Although it may sound like it, I'm not actually saying that all these foods are bad and should be banned. Who can doubt that chocolate, like alcohol, is one of God's good gifts? But it can be misused. After all, a treat is something you have occasionally. There was a time when hot water was a real treat; now most of us take it for granted. (I'm sure this is a good thing and I'm not advocating daily cold showers.) When the supply of sweets, cakes, biscuits and crisps is so plentiful that it's taken for granted, it stops being a treat and starts to be a problem.

It's not just a question of your child's health *now*, although that is, of course, important. Future health depends on learning to make good food choices. Habits developed in childhood are crucial. And if your child gets used to eating lots of sugary, fatty and salty foods now, it won't help at all.

 Top Tip: *Slowly sucking a lollipop damages teeth more than quickly chomping chocolate.*

Perhaps you know this already, but feel as though you're fighting a losing battle.

Here are ten ways to win with sweets and treats:

1. Feed your child well *before* setting off for the supermarket (and don't forget to eat something yourself). It's bad enough taking a child past rows of tempting sweets; it's worse if the child is hungry.
2. When you go out, take a snack (such as breadsticks or a banana) and produce it when your child is behaving well.
3. Try to avoid using sweets, biscuits or crisps as a reward – particularly a reward for eating other things. You don't want to send the message, 'You eat up those nasty vegetables and you can have some lovely sweets.'
4. Reward your child in other ways (such as playing a game or allowing a session on the computer).
5. If your child has grandparents who are, quite naturally, keen to give treats, suggest that there are lots of things that would be more helpful than sweets (such as small books, drawing pads or trips to the park).
6. Treat your toddler to tasty snacks such as vegetable sticks or yoghurt with fruit. There's no need to get a very young child hooked on sweets and crisps. Tastes and food choices are habits; you're in control of these early snacks.
7. Don't try to protect your child from sweets altogether. Unless you move to a desert island, sweets will be discovered sooner or later (sooner if there are any older brothers or sisters). Banning sweets may make them more attractive.
8. Decide what sweets and processed snacks you are happy for your child (and other members of the family) to have and don't keep any others in the house. Adults make life much harder for themselves by stocking up with sweets, biscuits, cakes and crisps – and then trying to resist them!
9. Ration sweets and develop a routine. Eating sweets at mealtimes is less damaging to the teeth than eating them

between meals. Also, it's not just the amount of sugar that's important, but how long it's in contact with the teeth: sucking a lollipop is worse for the teeth than quickly chomping through a chunk of chocolate. Our girls, aged seven and ten, choose two small sweets from a jar at the end of their evening meal, and on Saturdays they're allowed to spend some of their pocket money on extra sweets.

10. Relax! Sweets and crisps may not be the best food choices, but if they are just a tiny part of a big balanced diet, there's no reason why your child shouldn't enjoy them as treats.

Party Policy

Your child is having a birthday party and lots of little friends are coming. You're trying to bring your child up to understand that food can be fun without being full of fat, or fluorescent, sickly and devoid of any nutritional value. So, do you toe the party line and cover the tables with all the expected fare: crisps, sausage rolls, jellies, iced cakes and sweets? Or do you serve sensible food at the risk of being a party-pooper and disappointing lots of little guests?

The truth is, no matter how delighted children are to confront a mountain of colourful fat and sugar, they can't eat that much of it without feeling queasy. And you don't want to give them gastric grief. Of course you'll offer some traditional party foods; after all, your child doesn't have a birthday every day (some adults don't even have one every year). But the main thing is for the food to look colourful, festive and special.

Food doesn't have to be bad to look good. Here are some suggestions:

★ Cut brightly coloured vegetable sticks from peppers (red, green and yellow), carrot and cucumber, and offer as dunks for dips.

★ Give each child a little pot containing a tasty dip (or children will contaminate a communal dip with the nibble-dunk-dribble-dunk cycle).

★ Break some breadsticks into shorter lengths, and serve in little bowls as nibbles.

★ Dry-cook some pappadums on a paper towel in the microwave oven (e.g. 40–60 seconds on high power) and break into manageable pieces – a good alternative to crisps.

★ Serve toasted triangles of wholemeal pitta bread with mackerel pâté or dips such as hummus or tzatziki.

★ Make miniature sandwiches (some with white bread, some with brown and perhaps some with both) using fillings that are easily cut, such as fruit spreads, and thin ham or cheese.

★ For extra fun, use a shape cutter to produce bite-size sandwiches.

★ Pop some corn yourself (in a covered saucepan with just a little rapeseed oil) and serve in small bowls.

★ Enhance the spread with bowls of cherry tomatoes, grapes, Japanese rice crackers and assorted dried fruits.

★ Offer whole nuts if the children are over five, but make sure they don't play games like tossing peanuts and catching them in their mouths (a good way to get a peanut in the lung).

★ Include the traditional pineapple and cheese chunks on cocktail sticks (but watch out for little Sir Lance-a-lot among your guests, using the sticks as weapons).

★ Top small, plain biscuits with cream cheese and a piece of colourful fruit (such as mandarin, kiwi fruit or pineapple).

★ Cut and 'butter' (perhaps with an olive-oil spread) fruit scones, malt bread or even apricot and walnut bread (but put a warning flag on any foods containing nuts).

★ Serve reduced-sugar jellies made with added fruit.

★ Offer diluted fruit juices as well as the inevitable cola.

★ Make a cake with plaster of Paris for blowing out the candles, then serve a real, clean cake to the guests (just kidding – but it's not such a bad idea).

★ When the children are finally in bed, get fish and chips and put your feet up.

'Help! My Child's on Hunger Strike!'

What to Do When Your Child Won't Eat

Crying Over Spilt Milk

'Come on, Jack. You like baked bean bolognese,' said Sue, bringing a spoonful closer to Jack's lips. 'I don't know why I'm feeding you: you're two now; you're not a baby.'

Jack clenched his teeth and turned his head to one side.

'You won't grow up big and strong like Superman if you don't eat up your dinner,' said Sue. 'And there'll be no sweets later.'

Unmoved, Jack pushed the bowl away.

'Just have a little bit for Mummy,' Sue pleaded. 'Then you can have your chocolate cake for pudding.'

Jack took a swipe that would have sent the spoon flying if Sue hadn't withdrawn it in the nick of time.

'Stop that, Jack!' snapped Sue. 'I spent ages cooking this and it's delicious! Think of all the children who are starving. All you've got to do is open your mouth!'

Brian could see this wasn't getting them anywhere.

'Come on, big boy,' said Brian. 'Do you want to play "bombers" with Daddy again?'

Jack's face seemed to light up at this proposal. Brian went over to a corner of the room and stuck his arms out to simulate an aeroplane. Then, making a curious nasal sound, he veered from side to side across the room, getting ever closer to Jack who looked quite delighted by now.

'If only I had a video camera to hand,' thought Sue. 'Brian's colleagues at the bank would never believe this if I told them. And it must be worth £500 from *You've Been Framed*.'

Swooping dramatically over Jack's bowl, Brian collected a bolognese bomb in the spoon and successfully deposited it in Jack's gaping mouth. All went quiet. There was no explosion, but there was a nasty squelching sound and a lot of mess as Jack spat the delicious deposit back out of his mouth.

'That went like a bomb,' said Sue, wiping Jack's mouth.

'I'm not doing this for fun, you know,' replied Brian. 'Now look, Jack, you can have one more air raid, but if there's any nonsense this time, there'll be trouble!'

Brian positioned himself in the corner, ready for his mission. This time, arms outstretched, he swooped straight towards Jack's bowl. As he reached for the spoon, Jack thrust the bowl forward, knocking over his milk which splashed across the table and started pouring onto the floor.

'That's it!' shouted Brian, storming out of the room. 'We have the same thing every mealtime! I've had enough!'

Tears formed in Sue's eyes as she started mopping up the

milk. 'What are we going to do with you, Jack?' she wept. 'You've got to eat something or you'll waste away.'

Starvation Stunts Your Growth

Jack's case is not at all unusual and similar scenes take place in thousands of homes every day. But here's some good news. I'm happy to tell you that, after a little advice and support, mealtimes were transformed in Jack's home and his parents no longer have any anxieties about his eating.

It's quite normal for toddlers to refuse food. Whether this becomes a huge problem or not largely depends on the way it is handled.

Worried parents often come to see me complaining that their child 'won't eat'. Understandably, the parents are concerned that their obstinate offspring will starve or, at the very least, become seriously malnourished. In the great majority of cases, however, plotting the height and weight on a chart confirms completely normal growth. How can this be?

Jack's parents were puzzled when I showed them the evidence that he was slightly above the average height and weight for

his age – just as he had been six months previously. Sue and Brian couldn't understand how Jack could maintain a textbook pattern of growth without eating. But when I asked Sue to keep a diary of everything Jack ate and drank, it became clear that he was getting all the calories he needed, one way or another. If he hadn't touched his meal, Sue was only too pleased to get some milk, crisps or biscuits into him a bit later on.

You see, unlike a prisoner on hunger strike, toddlers are not interested in starving themselves. In fact, research shows that, as long as food is available, they are very good at making sure they get enough.

 Top Tip: *You can't force toddlers to eat – but you try stopping them when they're hungry!*

But there's something else that toddlers are very good at: winding up their parents. Toddlers eat when they feel hungry – not when it's expected of them. It didn't take Jack long to discover that refusing a meal won him tremendous care and concern from his parents. He could be ignored all morning while his mother got on with her chores, but as soon as he refused his lunch, Sue focused all her attention on him, confirming that he was, after all, at the centre of her universe. For sheer entertainment, the rewards of food refusal were hard to beat: how else could he get his father to become an aeroplane and make animal noises?

Giving lots of attention to your child's behaviour is the best way to make sure the behaviour is repeated.

The Solution

The first and absolutely essential step to solving Sue and Brian's problem was to convince them that Jack would not allow himself to starve. This meant they could ignore him completely when he didn't eat and they could get on and enjoy their own food. Mealtimes would last about half an hour. Anything Jack hadn't eaten at the end of that time was simply cleared away without comment. If his plate of food was untouched, it could be put in the fridge and served at the next meal.

Sue and Brian learnt the importance of giving Jack attention when he did eat well. They would look at him, smile, talk to him and praise him.

The hardest part, Sue found, was completely ignoring Jack, and showing no sign of concern whatsoever, when he didn't eat. It was only possible when she was satisfied that he would come to no harm. Of course, it was essential that visitors, such as Sue's mother, obeyed the same rules.

Jack was given two snacks in the day – the first between breakfast and lunch, and the second between lunch and the evening meal. There were no extra snacks if he refused his meal. Typical snacks would be chopped fruit (such as banana or peeled apple) or mini-sandwiches with a cup of milk. In the past, Jack could always fill up with extra milk between meals; now he was allowed two cups of milk a day and the rest of the time he was given water to drink.

No matter how much fuss he made, Jack wasn't given any food until the next meal or snack was due. Sue found this tough at first – especially when his bid for a bag of crisps involved screaming, stamping and sprawling on the floor. However, Jack soon got the message: food is available for a

Sample Menus for a Toddler

If you remember the four important food groups, planning a balanced menu is easy. Here are some examples:

Day 1	Day 2
Breakfast • Shredded Wheat Bitesize with raisins and milk • Apple slices • Cup of milk	**Breakfast** • Scrambled egg on toast • Pieces of pear • Cup of milk
Morning snack • Bread fingers with peanut butter* • Cup of water	**Morning snack** • Breadsticks with cheese • Cup of water
Lunch • Cheese on toast with tomato slices • Mixed bean salad • Yoghurt with added banana slices • Cup of water	**Lunch** • Tuna with sliced orange • Rice salad • Grapes • Cup of water
Afternoon snack • Carrot sticks • Piece of flapjack • Cup of water	**Afternoon snack** • Sugarsnap peas • Malt bread • Cup of water
Dinner • Chicken and vegetable casserole with potato • Rice pudding • Cup of milk	**Dinner** • Spaghetti Bolognese (lean mince) and sweetcorn • Strawberries with fromage frais • Cup of milk

> *Choose peanut butter containing nothing but peanuts with no added salt (available from health food shops). Avoid peanut products until your child is three if you have allergies in the family.

limited period only, and the best thing to do at mealtimes is to eat. And, of course, because his tantrums were never rewarded with food or attention, they soon stopped.

Jack still gets all the calories he needs for normal growth, but his diet is now more balanced. Mealtimes are much more relaxed – and so are Brian and Sue!

> **Top Tip:** *It's amazing how many children who 'won't eat a thing' are growing completely normally.*

My Child Won't Eat Greens

Broccoli is delicious and very good for you. I thoroughly recommend it. But my personal enthusiasm is not enough to convince my nephew that he loves it too. Children, like adults, are entitled to dislike certain foods. Some children, particularly toddlers, take this to extremes and are frustratingly faddy.

So, should you insist that they clear the plate? If you do, you'll probably find the broccoli behind the radiator six months later. Food battles make the problem worse; they do nothing to help your child appreciate food – to learn that food is fun.

91

Top Tip: *Fighting your child over food will always make the problem worse.*

It's quite true that one extreme method that has been used to deal with food fads is to keep serving a food that the child rejects, and little else, until – as a result of sheer hunger – the problem food is eaten (but not necessarily enjoyed). After all, as we've seen, hunger will drive a healthy child to eat long before starvation looms. However, you shouldn't need to resort to such a drastic strategy. I recommend a far more relaxed approach.

Don't go out of your way to serve a food that your child dislikes. When introducing a new food, it is best to start with a small amount along with something that's a definite hit. If the new food is spurned, don't get upset. To avoid showing any concern, you may find it helpful to say something like, 'I expect you'll like it when you're a bit more grown up.' Try again a few weeks later.

Remember those four important food groups. If a food is rejected, simply choose others from the same group *next time* (but don't offer replacement foods at the same meal). If broccoli is banished, there are lots of other options in the fruit and vegetable group. Mind you, unpopular vegetables can often be served in disguise – for example, in a pasta sauce. Make sure that your child has something from all four groups every day. Chips, baked beans and banana custard (made with real banana) might not have been your first choice but you've covered the four main groups.

Here are ten tips, tried and tested, to help you handle a faddy eater:

1. Eat together as a family whenever possible. Sit at the table, have the TV off and let your child see that you enjoy eating.
2. Don't get angry or plead with your child to eat. At the end of the meal (maximum thirty minutes), take uneaten food away without showing any concern.
3. Don't worry if a young child plays with the food; it's all part of a learning process and you can't expect adult manners from a toddler. I'm not suggesting you should sit there and be pelted with porridge. If behaviour's that extreme, simply take the food away. Don't get worked up.
4. When your child eats well, smile, praise and pay plenty of attention. Don't reward unwelcome behaviour with attention, and when your child isn't eating, simply talk to others at the table (but not about your child).
5. Provide regular meals and snacks. A toddler who has to wait for a late meal may be too irritable or tired to eat it.

SERVE SMALL PORTIONS — YOU CAN ALWAYS GIVE A SECOND HELPING.

6. When meals are rejected, don't give any *extra* food or milk between meals.

7. Whenever possible, avoid highly processed items such as manufactured cakes and biscuits, crisps and sweet drinks. These are high in calories and low in nourishment.

8. Give your child three-quarters of a pint of milk a day (whether as a drink or in food). After that, give water to drink: unlike 'juice', it's kind to teeth and won't fill your child with 'empty calories'.

9. Don't dump a daunting pile of food in front of your child. Serve small portions. If you get a clean plate, you can dish out plenty of praise and offer a second helping.

10. When children are involved in the preparation of food, they're more likely to eat it. Whenever possible, allow your child to 'help'.

 Top Tip: *If your child dislikes a food, simply choose a replacement from the same food group – at the next meal.*

My Child's Not Growing

We've seen that most of the children who 'won't eat' turn out to be growing normally; they're getting all the calories they need one way or another. But what if your child isn't growing so well?

When Timothy was two and a half, his dad, Jon, who was now a single parent, brought him to my surgery. Jon was obviously worried. He explained that Timothy had never had a big appetite, but now he was hardly eating at all. At the age of eighteen months, he had been admitted to hospital with an attack of wheezing, and he had been using inhalers for asthma ever since. He looked a little skinny.

I checked his height and weight and plotted them on the charts in his child health record book. Figure 2 shows Timothy's weight chart. His weight was on the tenth centile, which means that 10 per cent of boys of the same age would weigh less than Timothy. This put him comfortably within the normal range for weight.

But when we looked at previous records of his weight, it turned out that Timothy had been on the 25th centile at the age of two; and when he was nineteen months, he was on the 50th centile! During the previous 11 months, because he hadn't been gaining weight, he'd dropped from average weight to the bottom 10 per cent.

I examined Timothy and, in every other respect, he seemed healthy but we monitored him carefully to make sure that his asthma was well controlled. I discussed the problem with a health visitor who arranged to call on the family at a mealtime.

The meal was mayhem. The atmosphere was tense from the start and Jon became increasingly stressed as he begged Timothy to eat something. When this didn't work, he resorted to threatening Timothy with a range of sanctions from 'no sweets' to 'no birthday presents'. Finally, out of sheer desperation, he attempted to force-feed him. The health visitor noted that Timothy always seemed to have a bottle of milk or juice with him.

This wasn't a problem that could be solved overnight. Over the next two months, the health visitor worked very closely

Figure 2

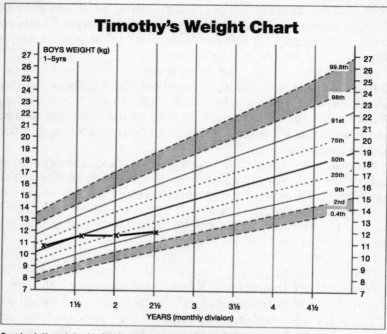

Reproduced with permission of the Child Growth Foundation. Separate charts are available for girls and boys, for all ranges.

with Jon and Timothy. The first step was to identify all the problems and to help Jon to understand where things were going wrong. A structured programme of change was agreed but Jon needed a lot of support to put it into practice. Timothy's bottle had to go: all drinks were given in a cup – water whenever he wanted it, and milk or water at mealtimes.

Top Tip: *Give your child water to drink between meals; too much milk or squash can spoil the appetite.*

Three meals and two snacks were provided every day at regular times. After a while, Jon learnt how to avoid rewarding Timothy with attention when he didn't eat. Timothy discovered that it was better to eat and realised there would be nothing but water available until the next meal or snack was due.

Timothy is growing normally now, the family is a lot happier, and the health visitor can call, even during a meal, without taking earplugs and protective clothing.

Failure to Thrive

'Failure to thrive' is what your chrysanthemums are suffering from if you return from holiday to find them lying down for a rest. The term is also used when a baby or child isn't growing adequately. The expression 'faltering growth' is sometimes preferred.

Traditionally, failure to thrive has been divided into two different sorts:

1. Organic. This means there is a physical condition such as cystic fibrosis or coeliac disease stunting the child's growth.
2. Non-organic. No physical cause can be found and it was often assumed that the child was being neglected in some way.

It turns out that this division into two distinct groups isn't very helpful. Even when there is a physical problem, poor growth usually comes down to the fact that the child isn't getting enough nourishment. In Timothy's case, the admission to hospital and the onset of asthma almost certainly contributed to his poor growth, but this is because they played a part in the development of feeding problems. And where there isn't a medical condition, it's very unusual to find that the poor nutrition results from abuse or neglect. Usually, parents are trying everything they can think of to get more calories into their child.

Parents may be burdened with a sense of failure when their children aren't growing as expected. A diagnosis of 'failure to thrive' may increase that burden; perhaps 'faltering growth' is less emotive. Whatever you call it, it's important to identify the problem as soon as possible so it can be put right.

The key to recognising a growth problem is to plot accurate weight (and height) measurements on a centile chart (see Figure 2 on page 96). You may have suitable charts in your child health record book. If in doubt, ask your health visitor.

> **Top Tip:** Plotting height and weight on a centile chart is the best way to check your child's growth.

How Often Should I Weigh My Child?

If you don't weigh often enough, you won't notice a growth problem. On the other hand, weighing too frequently achieves nothing but anxiety. A thriving baby piles on the pounds at first, but weight gain naturally slows down in the second year of life. So as your child grows, less frequent weighing is needed. Table 7 gives you a guide.

Table 7

Age	Weigh Every
1–3 months	2–4 weeks
3–12 months	1–3 months
1–2 years	3–6 months
Over 2 years	6–12 months

Scales should, of course, be accurate and it's reasonable to expect that they will be up to scratch at the child health clinic run by your GP and health visitor. It's helpful to use the same scales each time. Babies should be weighed naked. An older child can be weighed without shoes in light clothing; it's no good if he goes as Tarzan one time and Thomas the Tank Engine the next!

Growing Problem? Help Is at Hand

If you are unhappy with your child's growth pattern, the first thing to do is to talk it through with your health visitor or GP. It may well be that following the tips in this section, together with support from your health visitor, will be enough to get back on track. Any doubts about your child's physical health should be discussed with your doctor.

 Top Tip: *If you are unsure about your child's growth pattern, have a chat with your health visitor or GP.*

With feeding difficulties, the secret of successfully turning the corner is to break out of the vicious cycle of anxiety leading to more chaotic mealtimes.

Sometimes families need professional help to achieve this. Filming mealtimes with a video camera is one way of showing parents what's going wrong and how their own responses need to change in order to improve their child's eating behaviour. A plan of action is agreed but families need continuing support while they make the necessary changes.

So, if you feel that your toddler has really got you cornered, it's time to get help!

Just Puppy Fat?

<u>Overweight - A Growing Problem</u>

We are all pleased to see our bonny baby gaining weight. And quite right, too. It's a sign that all is well.

Babies grow at a remarkable rate in the first year and a normal one-year-old will weigh three times his birth weight. Then things slow down. This is just as well because if you carried on trebling your weight every year, by the age of six you would weigh two-and-a-half tons!

Mind you, it is all too easy to put on excess weight by the age of six. With the rapid growth of the first year behind them, toddlers briefly taunt their parents with the pretence that they are starving themselves to death, but they are far more likely to end up overweight. The number of seriously overweight six-year-olds has doubled in the last ten years.

There is an epidemic of obesity – not just in the UK but in other industrialised countries as well. While many other health statistics have improved, the proportion of men and women who are seriously overweight has gone on increasing. Overweight adults are much more likely to suffer from diabetes, high blood pressure and heart disease – not to mention breathing problems, gallstones, arthritis, hernias and social difficulties. Sadly, the obesity epidemic is now affecting our children too, and fat children are likely to become fat adults.

Hannah's Heartache

'Now, have you put your name on your homework, Hannah?' asked Mrs Jelly, bringing the car to a stop outside the school gates.

Hannah pulled a worksheet from her school bag and read the words 'Hannah Jelly' at the top.

'Why did you have to marry a man with such a silly name, Mum? I hate being called "Jelly".' Hannah reflected that she would much rather be called 'Smith'; having the surname 'Jelly' made it so easy for her classmates to taunt her with names like 'Jelly belly'. But deep down, she knew that, whatever her name was, children would find ways to tease her about being overweight.

'If I hadn't married your father, I couldn't have had *you*, darling,' replied Mrs Jelly.

'Exactly! It would be much better for me if I hadn't been born,' complained Hannah.

'Nonsense, darling. Anyway how could it be better for *you* if *you* hadn't been born? You wouldn't exist so you couldn't benefit.'

Hannah was a bright eleven-year-old, but she was in no

mood for a philosophy lesson. Today was Wednesday. She hated Wednesdays. Last week wasn't so bad because Mrs Jelly had written a note to excuse her from PE. This morning, though, Hannah had completely failed to convince her mum that dropping a Furby on her foot had caused serious injury.

'Go on, darling, or you'll be late!'

Hannah got out of the car.

'Oh, I forgot my purse!' said Hannah, stopping herself from closing the car door just in time.

A day at school without her purse was unthinkable. It was her survival kit. First, it contained enough money to buy a bag of crisps and a chocolate bar from Nicholas Hughes who was willing to part with his packed lunch – for the right price. Secondly, it held her coveted collection of bug cards; swapping cards with Sarah Pumphrey during lunch break would get her out of any energetic playground games. Not that she was ever picked for team games, but having something else to do saved her the embarrassment of being left out.

Mrs Jelly picked up Hannah's pink purse from the car seat and threw it gently in her direction. 'Catch!' Hannah extended her hand, but the purse landed on the pavement. 'What did you do that for?' moaned Hannah, bending awkwardly to pick up the purse. 'You know I can't catch.'

'I'm not surprised you're a bit boss-eyed after watching so much television,' retorted her mum. 'You were slumped in front of that box from tea till bedtime last night! Now, off you go, darling. It's twenty to nine.'

Hannah closed the car door and waved her mum goodbye. Turning round to face the school, she almost bumped into Jeremy Pringle, who must have been standing just behind her.

'Watching too much telly, Jelly?' he quipped. 'Never mind.

You'll soon work off some of that blubber. We're doing a cross-country run this afternoon!'

'Oh no,' thought Hannah, reaching for a comforting mint. 'Not being born must be better than this.'

The Energy Equation

Why was Hannah overweight? There's a simple answer and a complicated one.

If you were to ask why a business went bust, the simple answer could be that there was more money going out than coming in. That's simple and accurate. If you put the same question to a business analyst, you might get a lengthy report identifying lots of factors from a rude receptionist to a silly special offer.

In the same way, lots of factors in Hannah's life contributed to her problem. Genetics, family relationships and the school timetable all played their part. But the simple fact is, she carried on gaining weight because more energy was coming in than going out. She was taking in more food energy (calories) than she was using up with her day-to-day activity. All the spare calories were stored and she was growing fatter. You can't escape the energy equation:

| Energy intake (food and drink) | − | Energy expenditure (activity and metabolism) | = | Energy stored (fat and glycogen) |

Hannah was not an energetic child. She was driven to and from school; she did her best to avoid having to run around; she didn't enjoy games and felt silly because she had never become skilled at catching or kicking a ball. Hannah's favourite activities at home were watching TV and playing on the computer. Occasionally she would read. Of course, the less exercise Hannah did, the less she enjoyed it when she was forced into it at school. PE was only once a week, but she often managed to get out of that.

 Top Tip: _Learning good habits now can save your child from a lifetime of misery._

She didn't need a lot of food to fuel her inactive lifestyle. So adding high-calorie extras such as crisps, chocolate and sweets was asking for trouble.

The Obesity Epidemic

More and more children, like Hannah, are having to cope with being seriously overweight. Why?

We know from the energy equation (page 104) that children must either be eating and drinking more calories, or expending less energy (or perhaps both).

Here are a few reasons why some children may take in more calories nowadays:

- Manufactured snack foods – loaded with fat and sugar – are more abundant.
- Canned sugary drinks are widely available – even from school vending machines – and thirst is driven by high-salt snacks like crisps.

105

- More choice in school lunches: children choose chips.
- Powerful advertising for high-calorie food and drink targets children.
- Fast-food outlets specialising in high-fat foods appeal to children and young people.
- Many restaurants have children's menus offering carefully selected products – laden with fat and sugar.

 Top Tip: *High-salt snacks such as crisps will increase your child's thirst for high-sugar drinks like cola.*

Here are some reasons for children getting less exercise these days:

- We all walk less and use transport more.
- Many children are taken to and from school by car, partly because of parental concerns about safety.
- Escalators and lifts save our legs in public places.
- Labour-saving devices from the washing machine to the automatic car-wash have reduced the number of energetic chores that children are asked to help with. (When did your child last mangle the washing?)
- Children spend hours in front of computer and TV screens.
- Central heating may encourage us to be sluggish instead of moving around to keep warm.
- Some children don't have easy access to open spaces for recreation.
- Schools have reduced the time spent on PE.

The evidence points to reduced activity in children, rather than increased calorie consumption, as the key change underlying the obesity epidemic. In fact, average calorie intake has gone down – but not enough to compensate for less active lifestyles. Undoubtedly, spending long hours slumped in front of the TV, bombarded by adverts for children's high-energy foods, is no help at all.

Over a quarter of eleven- to sixteen-year-olds watch TV for more than four hours a day. And remote-control technology even spares them any exertion in changing channels.

But the problem starts much younger than this – perhaps even in the playpen.

How Much Exercise Should My Child Have?

Children should take part in moderately intense physical activity for at least an hour every day. That doesn't mean that they should do a one-hour exercise session each day! But the energetic activities in a child's day should add up to *at least* an hour's worth.

 Top Tip: Your child should spend at least an hour a day on energetic activities.

More than a third of our children aged between two and seven in England and Wales are not reaching this recommended activity level. According to a report released by the British Heart Foundation (BHF) in June 2000, primary schools in England

107

and Wales reduced by more than one half the time allocated to PE in the previous five years. And our secondary schools apparently devote less time to PE than anywhere else in Europe.

'Moderately intense physical activity' could include:

- playing active games
- brisk walking
- riding a bicycle
- swimming
- dancing
- washing the car!

This level of activity makes you puff and pant a little, but you can still shout at your playmates or hold a conversation (unless your face is under water).

It's also a good idea to make sure your child is including, at least twice a week, activities which particularly help to build strong muscles and bones. Suitable examples for a young child would be jumping and climbing (but not up a twenty-foot tree).

My Child Seems OK, So Why Bother about Exercise?

All these energetic activities are great fun. Playing computer games can be fun too, but physical activity is essential to your child's health and happiness – now and in the future.

By being active, your child will be building better bones, muscles and blood vessels; but there are huge social and emotional benefits too. If Hannah had learnt basic ball skills as a young child – or even how to ride a bike – she could have played much more confidently with her peers. And playing games is a natural way to ward off anxiety – for young and old alike.

Inactive children are missing out – and they're on the road to obesity, diabetes and heart disease. Many of them are already overweight.

Could My Child Be Overweight?

The best way to keep track of your child's growth pattern is to plot accurate height and weight measurements on a centile chart (see Figure 2 on page 96). No need to go mad though: after the age of two, a measurement every six to twelve months is ideal.

The 50th centile is average. If your child has an average height and weight, that's fine. But there's no reason why anyone should be average. Whether on the 25th or 98th centile, a normal growth curve is parallel to the centile lines on the chart.

Only 1 in 400 children are above the 99.6th centile or below the 0.4th centile; if your child's measurements are near the top or bottom centiles, discuss this with your doctor. Also seek advice if the growth curve is crossing centile lines instead of running parallel to them.

Ideal weight, of course, depends on height. A skinny giant will weigh more than a fat dwarf. So you can be reassured that your child is not overweight if height and weight measurements are on the same centile – whether it's the 9th or the 90th. On the other hand, a child who is on the 90th centile for weight but only the 50th centile for height, is 20 per cent heavier than expected and this is overweight.

Fighting Fat

It's far easier to prevent problems by applying the guidelines in this book from the earliest days than it is to put things right in a child who is already overweight.

If your child is overweight, remember the energy equation. By improving food habits and increasing activity, aim to keep your child's weight steady while height catches up. Of course, the whole family will benefit from eating better food and adopting an active lifestyle.

 Top Tip: If your child is overweight, apply the energy equation to keep weight steady while height catches up.

Here are ten tips to help your child (and family) enjoy food without getting fat:

1. Don't start solids too early. Four to six months is ideal and earlier weaning can get a baby off to a bad start.
2. Whenever possible, avoid processed foods – such as convenience meals and desserts, processed meat products, pies, pastries, cakes, biscuits and crisps – that are loaded with fat or sugar or both.
3. Give your child healthy snacks such as carrot sticks, or sugarsnap peas, or pieces of apple, pear or banana.
4. Aim for five portions of fruit and vegetable a day (e.g. two pieces of fruit and three servings of vegetables) for each member of the family.
5. Use wholegrain breads and cereals (such as breakfast cereals, muesli, rice and pasta) but don't overload a toddler with high-fibre foods (see pages 48–9).
6. Use skimmed milk (or semi-skimmed if you must) for everyone in the family aged five and over. If you're using whole milk at the moment, adapt gradually by increasing the proportion of skimmed milk.
7. Cut down on fat. The spreading fats (butter, margarine, and reduced-fat spread) are often unnecessary: serve toast and fruit spread without the layer of fat. When you do use spreading fats, spread them thinly. Choose lean meat and cut off visible fat. Dry-fry, grill or steam but avoid frying in added oil or fat. Keep chips down to once a week at most.
8. Cut down on sugar. Don't add sugar to drinks and cereals. Ration confectionery (e.g. two small sweets after tea on weekdays, and extra sweets after lunch on Saturday). Not only is it much better for teeth to confine sweets to

mealtimes, it also curbs the influx of unwanted calories.

9. Check food labels. Go for the products with less than 5 g of fat in 100 g. Avoid items with lots of added sugar, such as fizzy drinks, fruit in syrup (instead of natural juice), and sugar-coated breakfast cereals.

10. Don't insist that your child clears the plate; let eating be guided by appetite. Repeatedly using phrases like, 'Eat it all up and show me how much you love your Mummy', or using food as a reward, is asking for trouble in years to come.

Here are ten ways to get your family moving:

1. Use the car less. If possible, walk to school with your child. Could a 'walking school bus' be organised in your area, so that children can walk safely in a supervised group?

2. When you travel by bus, get off earlier – but preferably when it's stopped – and walk the rest of the way.

3. Use stairs instead of escalators or, at least, walk on the escalator. (Use lifts if you have a pram or buggy, otherwise leave the lifts free for those who need them.) Don't keep your child in a buggy more than necessary – the exercise of running after a toddler will do you good.

4. If you're a good mover, put on some music and teach your child to dance. If you're not, let your child teach you.

5. Walk with your child when you post letters, visit nearby friends, shop at the local store, or exercise the dog. If the family pet is a gerbil, at least walk with your child to buy pet food.

6. Let your child help you with energetic chores such as washing the car, sweeping the path, or raking the lawn –

even if the jobs do take you twice as long!

7. If you have a garden, let your child invite friends round to play. If you don't have a garden, get very friendly with families who do!

8. Set firm limits on the time your child spends watching TV or using the computer – not just so you can get on the Internet, but to allow time for energetic recreation. Playing active games with your child does you both good.

9. Children are naturally keen to learn, and acquiring new skills boosts their confidence. So teach your child to catch, kick (a ball), cycle, skate and swim. If necessary, book some lessons (and why not join the class as well?).

10. Make use of local facilities (e.g. park, swimming pool, community centre). Activity camps can be excellent and, if you can afford to, it's well worth sending your child to one in the school holidays. Your child will benefit too.

 Top Tip: _Eating well and adopting an active lifestyle will do the whole family good._

Watch Out! There's Food About!

How To Avoid Poisoning Your Family

One evening, when I was working as a doctor in a children's hospital, three-year-old Aaron was brought to see me in his mother's arms. The mother had tears in her eyes. At first glance, it looked as if Aaron was asleep, but it soon became clear that he was unconscious.

'How long has he been like this?' I asked Aaron's mother. Bit by bit the story unfolded. Aaron had been suffering from diarrhoea for a couple of days – severe, watery diarrhoea. Aaron's mother explained that she had been treating him with a special medicine for diarrhoea. She showed me the bottle; it was a kaolin mixture. Despite this, Aaron's diarrhoea got worse rather than better.

Then his behaviour changed, according to his mother. He started turning on the bath taps and trying to drink the water. She thought this was very odd, so she stopped him. Before she knew it, he was becoming drowsy. She got worried

115

and rushed him round to the hospital.

Aaron was severely dehydrated and, of course, we wasted no time in setting up a drip to give him intravenous fluids. It wasn't that simple. He needed repeated blood tests to get the fluid balance right and he very nearly didn't make it. Fortunately, a few days later, he was well enough to go home. If treatment had been started any later, it would have been a different story.

Laboratory examination of a stool sample detected the food-poisoning bug salmonella. It turned out that this had come from a chicken that hadn't been properly cooked. There was still some in the fridge waiting to be eaten!

Food is dangerous stuff. It can kill you. It very nearly killed Aaron. Then again, Aaron certainly wouldn't have lived three years without it. And not only is food essential to life, it's also one of life's great pleasures. But it needs to be treated with respect.

I KNEW I SHOULDN'T HAVE ASKED MUM FOR 'DINNER AND MAKE IT SNAPPY'...

FOOD CAN BE DANGEROUS STUFF

Food Poisoning

Food poisoning is extremely common. As every family doctor knows, official statistics don't reflect the size of the problem because so many cases go unreported.

 Top Tip: Food poisoning is rife, but you can take simple steps to protect your family.

What causes food poisoning?

Most food poisoning is caused by nasty bacteria (such as salmonella, campylobacter and E. coli) which can so easily contaminate our food. Other bugs (such as viruses and parasites) and toxic chemicals are often to blame as well.

If your beefburger looked a bit green and smelt of drains, you probably wouldn't eat it – let alone feed it to your child. The trouble is, food may look and smell fine but still be harmful.

What are the symptoms of food poisoning?

The usual symptoms are vomiting and diarrhoea resulting from inflammation in the stomach and bowel (gastroenteritis). Tummy pains – especially cramps coming just before a bout of diarrhoea – fever, headache and a general flu-like feeling are common as well.

How soon do the symptoms come on?

This depends on the cause of food poisoning. Some toxins (for example, from seafood) can make themselves felt within

117

minutes, while certain bacteria (such as the typhoid germ) may take a couple of weeks to kick in. In most cases symptoms start between twelve and seventy-two hours after eating contaminated food.

What should I do if my child has diarrhoea?

Fortunately, the illness is not usually as serious as Aaron's. If only Aaron's mother had understood the importance of giving extra drinks when diarrhoea occurs, to replace lost water, the crisis could have been avoided. Instead, she was relying on a medicine to stop the diarrhoea; this is dangerous – especially in children. It distracts you from the crucial task of giving plenty to drink.

 Top Tip: *If your child has diarrhoea, it's vital to give plenty of the right kind of drinks.*

For mild diarrhoea, water or diluted juice are suitable drinks. Better still, particularly when diarrhoea is more severe, are the rehydrating mixtures that are available from pharmacies. It is essential to follow the manufacturer's instructions – adding the right amount of water to the sachet or tablets. Correctly made up, these solutions are absorbed much better than water from a bowel inflamed by gastroenteritis. Don't use them for drinks when your child is well.

In some cases, cows' milk will worsen diarrhoea and vomiting so it is generally better to use non-milk drinks until things have settled. If you are breastfeeding your child, carry on – and give extra feeds – but make sure you drink plenty yourself.

A child who is producing three loose motions a day, and is drinking normally, is unlikely to become dehydrated. But if your child has frequent, watery diarrhoea, you must put enough rehydrating fluid in the top end to replace the output from the bottom. Of course, children can't be forced to drink something they don't like. It's just as well that rehydrating mixtures come in a range of flavours.

Should I starve my child during a tummy upset?

Be guided by your child's appetite which will probably be reduced to start with. Once hunger strikes, don't try to withhold food until diarrhoea has settled – which may take a week. Go carefully because eating will often trigger stomach cramps. You can start with a starchy food such as plain bread and don't forget to keep up the drinks.

What about vomiting?

Vomiting makes things more difficult – especially when every drink is immediately returned. This often happens at the start of the illness. It can't go on for long without causing dehydration. Fortunately, in most cases, persistent vomiting soon settles – even if it is followed by a week of diarrhoea. When vomiting is a problem, give tiny sips of fluid frequently. Licking an ice lolly is another way of drinking.

Production of plenty of pale urine is a sign that your child is drinking enough. When fluid is short, small amounts of dark urine are passed infrequently.

If your child is feverish, drowsy or unable to drink enough, consult your doctor.

What will my doctor do?
The first thing your doctor will do is to make sure it is safe to treat your child at home. Usually it is – as long as enough of the right drinks are given, as well as paracetamol for fever if necessary. Occasionally, hospital management is needed: it may be necessary to set up a drip and give fluid directly into a vein; also, as diarrhoea and vomiting can be caused by other diseases apart from food poisoning, some tests may be called for.

A fit young person may shrug off a dose of diarrhoea after a dodgy doner kebab, but food poisoning is more likely to be serious in vulnerable people, which includes babies and young children (as well as pregnant women, the elderly and those with poor immunity).

 Top Tip: *Food poisoning is bad enough for adults; it's more dangerous for young children.*

Your doctor may give you a form and a specimen pot and ask for a stool sample. There's no need to fill the pot with poo, which will often be liquid anyway. The main thing is to get a 'fresh' specimen to the laboratory; once you've collected a small sample, deliver it as soon as you can.

Is the infection likely to spread?
Yes. When one member of the family is suffering from diarrhoea or vomiting, everybody needs to be extra careful about hygiene. All hands must be thoroughly washed with soap and warm water after using the toilet and before preparing food or eating.

Children should not return to nursery or school until they have made a full recovery.

120

Make sure the toilet (including the flush handle) is thoroughly cleaned with disinfectant. Also clean the bathroom taps and door handles, and replace the towels.

When food poisoning is suspected, the local Environmental Health Service should be notified. Your doctor will certainly do this if the laboratory finds a food-poisoning bug in the stool sample.

As a result, you may be contacted by an environmental health officer. Even if your child is fit and well by then, the information you provide can help to identify the source of infection and protect other people from illness. It's very helpful if you make a record of everything your child ate in the three days before the illness. You will probably be asked about any recent travel abroad, and about any contact your child has had with animals and birds, or with people suffering from diarrhoea or vomiting.

Prevention is better

I think that's quite enough on diarrhoea and vomiting in a book about the joy of food. Mind you, writing or reading about gastroenteritis is nothing compared with having it. If you've ever had food poisoning, you certainly don't want it again and you won't want your child to get it either.

There are lots of important precautions you can take to protect your family. Here are ten tips to avoid tummy trouble:

1. *Check 'Use by' dates*

'Use by' dates are shown on perishable foods; these products may become unsafe after that date. It's best not to risk it – even if the product still looks and smells OK. (You can buy extra time, if the food is suitable for freezing, by putting it in the

WHAT MAKES YOU THINK THIS ALPHABET SOUP'S PAST ITS 'SELL BY' DATE?

THE ALPHABET'S IN OLDE ENGLISHE!

CHECK 'USE BY' DATES

freezer *before* the 'Use by' date.)

'Best before' dates are different and you don't have to be so strict about them. Even so, it's sensible to enjoy food at its best – long before it goes like old socks.

2. *Chill out*

Put chilled and frozen foods together in the shopping trolley (but make sure any raw meat or poultry is well wrapped in plastic bags to protect other items from contamination). Use a cool bag for a long journey home (especially in hot weather) and get food into the fridge or freezer as soon as possible.

3. Cool it

Use a fridge thermometer to make sure the coldest part of your fridge is below 5 °C (0–5 °C). Adjust the thermostat or defrost if necessary. Don't overload the fridge: unlike freezers (which work more efficiently when packed), fridges need the air to circulate; overloading produces pockets of warmer air. Don't put hot food in the fridge; cool it as fast as possible first – in the coolest part of the kitchen or in a sealed container under water. Don't leave the fridge door open any longer than you have to.

4. Beware poison!

Raw meat must be treated with caution. After all, if one drop of meat juice containing E. coli 0157 lands on ready-to-eat food, it can prove fatal. Keep raw meat, poultry or fish at the bottom of the fridge (in extra wrapping, even if pre-wrapped, or in a covered container). Use separate chopping boards and knives for raw meat and salad (or any other food that won't be cooked).

5. Clean up

Clean kitchen worktops and taps after preparing raw meat or poultry. Wash utensils, dishes and chopping boards thoroughly; use piping hot water with detergent, and rinse. A dishwasher is a huge help (and, although my wife is married to one, we've found an electric model even better). Ditch the dishcloth frequently: it's a fertile breeding ground for bacteria. Change tea towels and hand towels often.

6. Wash hands

This is one of the simplest ways to save lives. It is essential to wash hands thoroughly in warm soapy water before touching food, and after going to the toilet, or stroking the pet, or blowing your nose, or handling raw meat. Help your child to acquire the healthy habit of hand hygiene too. You will need to explain, more than once, that washing hands does not mean passing them under the tap and wiping the dirt on the towel.

 Top Tip: *Washing hands well is one of the simplest ways of saving lives.*

Cover cuts and grazes before preparing food; bacteria in infected wounds and boils can cause food poisoning.

7. Put the cat out

However put out your cat may be, pets must be kept away from worktops, tea towels, crockery and food (apart from their own, of course). Whether the beloved family pet is a parrot or a python, it is a ready source of food-poisoning bugs and has no place in the kitchen (unless thoroughly cooked).

8. Cook well

Many raw foods contain dangerous bacteria. A lot of chickens are contaminated with salmonella. In most cases, as long as the food is *thoroughly* cooked, this will be no problem. Don't stuff poultry, as this makes it harder to cook to the centre; some cooks continue to do it on the grounds that stuffing doesn't taste as good when cooked separately (but that's stuff and nonsense – a dose of salmonella enteritis has a way of changing your opinion).

124

Beware badly barbecued burgers and sausages – burnt outside but pink in the middle. Processed meat products are a particular hazard because germs can be spread through the product during manufacture. You might get away with eating a rare steak, as long as it's well cooked on the outside, but never accept a rare burger!

> **Top Tip:** Food can look and smell OK but still be harmful.

Always follow cooking instructions. Thoroughly defrost frozen meat and poultry before cooking. If you reheat food, make sure it's piping hot throughout.

9. Handle with care

Extra care is needed to avoid food poisoning in babies and toddlers because (like elderly people, those with poor immunity, and pregnant women) they are more vulnerable. So cook eggs until the white and the yolk are solid, and avoid foods (such as Hollandaise sauce) which contain uncooked eggs. Don't use unpasteurised milk. Vulnerable people, including pregnant women, should also avoid paté and soft ripened cheeses (Brie, Camembert and blue-vein varieties).

10. If in doubt, chuck it out!

It's better than chucking up. Get rid of mouldy food; I know it's tempting, but don't just cut off the mouldy bits because the mould penetrates invisibly into the food. Once opened, packaged foods can go off quickly. Don't keep food in opened cans: the tin may contaminate it. Discard food that's been left open to flies. Sooner throw away a bit of food than risk your family's health.

Out and About

Of course, if you eat out, you don't have the same control over the purchase, storage and preparation of food. Look out for telltale signs of poor hygiene. You may not be able to take microbiological samples from the kitchen or the food, but if the toilet's disgusting, you probably don't need to. Don't wait for marauding rats or cockroaches to frighten you off: the sight of unwrapped sandwiches and money in the same pair of hands should be enough. If you suspect very sloppy standards, alerting the Environmental Health Service could save someone from serious illness.

LOOK OUT FOR TELLTALE SIGNS OF POOR HYGIENE

'Could My Child Have a Food Allergy?'

Allergies and Additives –
Your Questions Answered

Anne was still in a state of shock when she brought her daughter, Chloe, to see me. Just four days earlier, on Chloe's thirteenth birthday, Anne thought her only daughter was going to die. She nearly did.

They had been enjoying a family celebration of Chloe's birthday in a local restaurant when Chloe was suddenly taken ill. She complained of tightness in her chest and difficulty breathing. The family were puzzled to see that her skin had become blotchy. In fact she looked dreadful and an ambulance was called.

Chloe got up from the table, wheezing and clutching her

chest. She went outside for some fresh air. Anne followed her. Despite the fresh air, Chloe got worse by the second; she collapsed into Anne's arms and started to lose consciousness. Anne was beside herself – desperate to help, but powerless. Moments before, her daughter had been happy and healthy; now she was fading away in her arms.

Fortunately the ambulance arrived very quickly. The paramedics immediately put an oxygen mask on Chloe's face and gave her an injection of adrenaline (epinephrine); this was followed by an injection of antihistamine. Chloe spent that night in intensive care, but rapidly made a full recovery.

Chloe had suffered a severe, overwhelming allergic reaction called anaphylaxis. Correct treatment was given just in time to save her life.

But what was she allergic to? It emerged that, although Chloe didn't realise she was allergic to nuts, she had discovered a long time ago that they could make her feel unwell, so she avoided them. As far as the family could remember, the last time Chloe ate nuts, she complained of discomfort in her lips followed by tummy pains and diarrhoea; she had certainly never had breathing problems in the past. But since then, to avoid any tummy upsets, they always made sure there were no nuts in Chloe's food.

Further investigation revealed that the restaurant had used nut butter in one of the dishes. Anne couldn't believe that such a trivial oversight had nearly killed her daughter.

Are Nuts Really Dangerous?

For most people nuts are delicious, nutritious and safe – a good source of protein as well as the more friendly unsaturated fats.

NUTS CAN BE DANGEROUS

But if you have a nut allergy, even minute quantities can be lethal. Lucretius (95–55 BC) was right when he said, 'One man's meat is another's poison.'

Peanuts are the most common culprits, although tree nuts such as brazils, almonds, hazelnuts and walnuts can also be to blame. Those who know they have a nut allergy, or a child with a nut

129

allergy, have to be constantly on their guard. Even food labels aren't always reliable as mere traces of nut protein in a product can have serious consequences. The biggest danger comes with eating outside the home; you can't rely on what a waiter tells you.

If you suspect that your child has had a bad reaction to nuts, discuss it with your doctor who can refer you to a specialised clinic for further assessment if necessary. People with severe nut allergy, or their parents, are sometimes provided with self-injectable adrenaline for use in emergencies and this is what I arranged for Chloe.

Your child is more likely to develop nut allergy if exposed to nut protein in infancy. This is why nuts and seeds (and products such as groundnut oil, peanut butter and tahini) are amongst the foods that should not be given to a baby under six months old. If you have allergies in your family (such as asthma, eczema and hay fever), it is wise not to give your child peanut products for the first three years, and to avoid eating peanuts yourself if you are breastfeeding.

Top Tip: *If you have allergies in your family, don't give your child peanut products for the first three years.*

In any case, whole nuts should not be given to children under five because of the risk of choking.

What Other Foods Can Cause Serious Allergic Reactions?

Catastrophic allergic reactions like Chloe's are usually the result of the body's immune system overreacting to foreign protein.

(The protein is called 'foreign' because the immune system senses that it doesn't belong in the body; I'm not suggesting British eggs are safer than French.)

Apart from nuts, the high-protein foods that are most likely to cause trouble are cows' milk, eggs, fish and shellfish.

Is There Anything I Can Do to Protect My Child From Food Allergies?

Yes. For a start, avoid giving your baby the problem protein foods (nuts, cows' milk, eggs, fish and shellfish), wheat (and other foods containing gluten) and citrus fruits (such as oranges) in the first six months (see Table 6 on page 68).

If you have allergies in your family, don't give your child peanut products (including unrefined groundnut oil) for the first three years. Also, with advice from your doctor or health visitor, you could wait longer than six months to introduce certain other foods. For example, you might be advised to wait until your baby is eight months or a year before giving general dairy products or mixing normal cows' milk with your baby's food. (Of course, you shouldn't give cows' milk as a drink until one year in any case.) But if you don't use dairy products, it's essential to replace them with other foods which provide enough calcium (see page 37). Your doctor may refer you to a dietitian.

Will Breastfeeding Help to Stop My Baby Getting Allergies?

Yes. Breastfeeding helps and if you manage to give nothing but breast milk for the first six months, so much the better. Solids should be started no earlier than four months and no later than six months; continue to breastfeed after starting solids if you can.

One problem is that some foreign proteins from your own diet, for example proteins in peanuts or cows' milk, can get into your breast milk. For this reason, some breastfeeding mothers with a family history of allergies choose to avoid eating dairy products, eggs, fish, shellfish, peanuts and even soya beans. (It's so much easier to be a dad.)

 Top Tip: *If you are breastfeeding, some proteins in your own diet could trigger allergy in your child.*

Of course, it's essential to maintain a balanced diet; do seek professional advice if you intend to make big changes.

If My Child Has an Unpleasant Reaction to a Food, Will It Show Up Straight Away?

Not necessarily. Serious allergic reactions like Chloe's are immediate and obvious. Less dramatic food intolerances can take anything from an hour to a few days to produce symptoms. This is why it can be so hard to link symptoms with the problem food.

At between six and nine months your baby benefits from being introduced to as many different foods, tastes and textures as possible. But always bring in one new food at a time and be on the lookout for any unpleasant reaction. After a couple of days, if all is well, add another new food.

What's the Difference Between Food Allergy and Food Intolerance?

The word 'allergy' is often used very loosely and some people even claim to be allergic to work! Technically, though, an allergic reaction involves the body's immune system. The army of cells and substances which protects us against infection by launching an attack on invading germs sometimes becomes oversensitive to other things such as a protein in food. The resulting allergic response will often cause minor symptoms (e.g. an itchy rash) but occasionally triggers life-threatening anaphylaxis as it did in Chloe's case.

'Intolerance' covers other unpleasant reactions to particular foods. If you can't tolerate the man next door, it's probably nothing to do with antibodies. In the same way, if milk or coffee or some other food upsets you, it doesn't necessarily have anything to do with your immune system. For example, a cup of milk could give you diarrhoea and wind because you lack the enzyme (lactase) needed to digest milk sugar (lactose). A genuine, chemical food intolerance causes symptoms even when the food is disguised; some reactions are psychological and don't occur in 'blind' tests. If your neighbour were cleverly disguised, you might find him quite agreeable.

How Else Can Food Intolerance Show Up?

It's fashionable to put all sorts of problems down to food intolerance. Proving the point is another matter – especially if you develop symptoms a couple of days after eating the guilty food.

Migraine, which is not uncommon in children, can be triggered by chemicals called amines in foods such as cheese,

133

chocolate and citrus fruit. There is even a 'hot dog headache'. This is not a canine complaint caused by leaving the dog in the family car on a hot day (which you must never do). It's a human affliction provoked by nitrates in some sausages. 'Chinese restaurant syndrome' is caused by a dose of monosodium glutamate from a Chinese meal: chest and arm pains soon after eating can mimic a heart attack; more commonly, nausea and headache set in sometime later. Monosodium glutamate can also trigger an asthma attack.

Top Tip: *Some food additives, such as nitrates and monosodium glutamate, cause unpleasant reactions in sensitive people.*

Coeliac disease is uncommon, but making the diagnosis can restore a very sick child to full health. People with coeliac disease are sensitive to gluten – a protein found in wheat, rye and some other cereals. They cannot absorb food properly because gluten damages the lining of the small intestine. Avoiding gluten solves the problem.

Like all family doctors, I often see children with urticaria (also known as nettle rash or hives). Parents are sometimes alarmed by the sudden appearance of itchy weals, but the rash doesn't usually last very long. An antihistamine, taken by mouth, may help to settle it. The condition is caused by release of histamine within the body, but it isn't usually possible to pinpoint the trigger. In some cases it is a reaction to food.

If you have a child who suffers badly from eczema, no doubt you would love to solve the problem by making a simple change in your child's diet. Attempts to do so are often disappointing. However, in one controlled trial, eczema improved in fourteen out of twenty young children after the removal of egg and milk from their diets. Wheat is another food which is sometimes linked with eczema.

Is It True That Food Intolerance Can Even Make You Deaf?

(Pardon?) Odd though it sounds, this is possible. Glue ear is a common cause of deafness in children. Sticky fluid collects in the middle ear cavity; the Eustachian tube connecting the middle ear to the back of the nose gets blocked; the adenoids are often enlarged. Now, I'm not saying that all this is simply explained by food intolerance, but in some children sensitivity to certain foods may well contribute to the congestion and production of mucus.

Matthew's mother was at her wits' end. Night after night, Matthew would wake up crying with earache. He'd been moved to the front of the classroom, but he still couldn't hear the teacher properly and his school work was suffering. There was a temporary improvement after an operation to remove his adenoids and insert grommets in his eardrums. But it all flared up again and they were back to square one. Then they consulted a nutritionist who recommended exclusion of wheat and dairy products from Matthew's diet. Like magic, his hearing returned and he's been fine ever since.

Of course, the sceptic will point out that glue ear is a condition that children grow out of. Perhaps Matthew was just about to improve anyway. You try telling his mother that! Her only regret is that she didn't discover his food sensitivities earlier.

"THE NUTRITIONIST SAYS BANANAS ARE MAKING HIM DEAF."

Is It True that Hyperactivity Is Due to Food Allergy?

Hyperactive children, who cannot sit still for a moment and create mayhem wherever they go, are very frustrating to deal with. They've been called many different things over the years: 'hyperactive' and 'hyperkinetic' are just two of the printable names. Nowadays, they are likely to be diagnosed as having 'attention-deficit hyperactivity disorder' (ADHD).

A popular theory

An American doctor, Benjamin Feingold, suggested back in 1975 that these children would improve on a special diet. The Feingold diet attempts to avoid foods containing artificial additives or salicylates (chemicals related to aspirin and found naturally in certain foods).

The trouble is, later researchers who carried out proper double-blind studies were unable to confirm Feingold's hypothesis. One problem is that a lot of 'difficult' children will improve if you put them on any special diet – simply in response to all the attention and concern that goes with it. Parents who believe that their child mutates into a monster after two squares of chocolate or a glass of fizzy orange may be quite right, but it's easy to be misled.

Katy and the cola

Katy was normally a quiet and sensible girl, her mother explained, but she became very silly if she had cola to drink. It turned out that Katy's normal drink at home was water. She only had cola when a friend came round or when she went to a party – or on some other occasion when there was every reason to get overexcited.

Although water is the ideal drink, I asked Katy's mother to try, for once, serving cola with Katy's lunch when the two of them were alone together. Katy was naturally curious about this special 'treat' but, her mother had to concede, she was calm and sensible throughout.

Feingold's diet cannot be recommended as a general solution to hyperactivity. But there is evidence that food sensitivity affects behaviour in some children. Elimination diets have been shown to help some children with a combination of overactivity and other symptoms suggestive of food sensitivity (such as rashes and rhinitis). It seems that tartrazine (E102) and benzoic acid (E210) are top of the list of ingredients affecting behaviour.

Top Tip: Tartrazine and benzoic acid are top of the list of additives that can affect behaviour.

Don't try putting your child on an elimination diet without professional advice. If it looks as though this approach is worth trying, your doctor will be happy to refer you to a dietitian.

Aren't Most Food Allergies Due to Additives?

No. Reactions to foods such as milk, eggs, fish, shellfish, nuts, soya and wheat are far more common than reactions to additives.

Should I Avoid E Numbers?

E numbers don't really deserve their shady reputation. After all, the 'E' is actually a merit award: it simply means that the additive has been accepted as safe throughout the European Union. Many are natural food ingredients such as E300 – added as an anti-oxidant to stop food going off and better known as vitamin C.

ABC of E numbers

Most food additives have been in use for a long time. Before an additive can be approved, it must be considered safe and necessary. Those with E numbers are approved throughout the European Union.

Additives may be:

1. natural substances, such as chlorophyll (E140) – a green pigment found in plants;
2. chemically identical to a natural substance but made in a laboratory, e.g. vanillin which occurs naturally in vanilla pods;
3. artificial, e.g. tartrazine (E102) – a man-made colouring used in soft drinks.

There are over 3,000 flavourings but they don't have E numbers. Flavour recipes are considered trade secrets. Although additives with similar functions are grouped together, they are not all numbered consecutively; there are only 43 permitted colours, not 81, even though they have numbers from 100 to 180.

Colourings (E100–E180)
Shoppers prefer colourful products, according to research by the food industry. Colourings are used to put back colour lost in processing. Some are natural (e.g. beetroot, chlorophyll, carotene, paprika) but 20 of the 43 colours are artificial. Tartrazine (E102), Sunset Yellow (E110) and Annatto (E160b) are known to cause reactions in some people. Only three colourings are allowed in baby foods and these also act as vitamins.

Preservatives (E200–E297)
Unless it is tinned, frozen, dried, pickled or preserved in lots of salt or sugar, any food with a long shelf-life is likely to contain a 'preservative'. The nitrites and nitrates (E249–E252) – which not only preserve 'cured' meats but also make them pinker – can cause reactions (e.g. 'hot dog headache'). Sulphur dioxide (E220) which is used to preserve dried fruit can provoke wheezing in some people with asthma.

Antioxidants (E300–E321)
These protect foods from reaction with oxygen in the air which turns fat rancid and changes the colour of foods (causing a cut apple to turn brown, for example). The group includes nature's own antioxidants, vitamins C and E. The gallates (E310–E312), BHA (E320) and BHT (E321) have been blamed for reactions in some people.

Emulsifiers, stabilisers, thickeners and gelling agents (E322–E495)
Additives in this group allow ingredients like oil and water to mix without separating, and improve the texture of foods. Plant gums, such as carob gum, are used as thickeners.

Sweeteners (E420–E959)
There are two main types of sugar substitute.

The intense sweeteners – such as aspartame (E951) and saccharin (E954) – are used in tiny quantities to add sweetness without calories, but are not allowed in foods specifically aimed at babies and young children. Saccharin was temporarily banned in the UK after it was linked with bladder cancer in male rats (but not in people). Aspartame is controversial because reports that it causes dizziness, headaches and visual disturbance have not been confirmed by scientific studies.

Sorbitol (E420) is a bulk sweetener – about half as sweet as table sugar. It's kind to teeth, but any significant quantity will probably give your child stomach cramps and diarrhoea.

There's no doubt, however, that some additives, including ones with E numbers, cause unpleasant reactions in a small minority of people – but many more people are upset by food itself.

Aren't Organic Foods Less Likely to Cause Allergic Reactions?

There's no evidence to support this idea. It's quite reasonable, if you can afford it, to buy organic fruit and vegetables because you want to avoid pesticide residues. Although it may not remove all traces of pesticide, it's wise to scrub fruits that can stand it (such as apples and pears) with a washing-up brush in warm water, before thoroughly rinsing under running cold water. If you buy organic produce, do the same to remove all that lovely organic manure.

What About Allergy Tests?

The idea that a simple test can tell you the foods that disagree with you is very attractive – especially to people who sell the tests.

Reputable allergy clinics do sometimes use skin tests and blood tests. Drops of liquid containing food extracts are placed on the forearm and the skin is pricked through each drop. A positive reaction shows up as a weal within twenty minutes. A blood sample can be analysed for antibodies to various food substances. These tests need to be interpreted very carefully. They can only throw light on cases of true allergy – not other causes of food intolerance. Also, someone with a tendency to allergies may have positive tests for foods which are not actually causing symptoms.

There's no shortage of other tests available if you have the money. Amie's mother was desperate to find out which foods were triggering Amie's eczema. So she was pleased to answer an advert for an allergy-testing service: all she had to do was to send her cheque with a sample of Amie's hair. But when the report came back, she was concerned to see the length of the list of foods which Amie was advised to avoid. She thought she had better seek a second opinion so she sent a further sample of Amie's hair to another 'clinic'. This time she received a completely different list of foods for Amie to avoid.

Other unorthodox tests are equally unreliable. In an investigation into the 'cytotoxic food test', a blood sample was split and sent to the *same* unit under two different names: different results were obtained although it was the same blood.

Top Tip: *Don't waste money on unreliable and misleading allergy tests.*

There is even a test that involves measuring your pulse rate while you eat different foods – the idea being that your heart rate goes up if you're allergic to the food. But then, it will probably also go up if you think about the cost of the test!

What Should I Do If I Think My Child Has a Food Allergy or Intolerance?

It's helpful to keep a dietary diary – making a record of what your child has to eat and drink as well as noting any symptoms. See your doctor about any significant symptoms. After all, problems you suspect are due to food sensitivity may actually have another cause; your doctor can help to sort out whether it's down to allergy or a lurgy!

Don't hesitate to see your doctor if you think your child has had a reaction to nuts or shellfish, even if the symptoms were mild. Sensitivity can build up (as it did with Chloe – see pages 127–8) leading to a more severe reaction in future. Your doctor may refer you to an allergy specialist.

For less serious problems, because laboratory tests don't provide the answer, it's usually necessary to make changes in the diet while monitoring symptoms. This is a minefield. For a start, it's easy to think you've eliminated something from your child's diet (such as cows' milk protein) and not realise you're still giving it as a hidden ingredient in some processed food or another. There is also the risk that you will end up giving your child an unbalanced diet. Your doctor will probably refer you to a dietitian.

Can Food Allergies Get Better?

Yes. One of the advantages of being a child is that a lot of things get better as you get older. About 8 per cent of children have food allergies in the first three years of life, but most of them have grown out of the problem by the age of five. Unfortunately, as a rule, nut allergies do not improve.

'Chicken Nuggets and Chips, Please, Mum!'

How to Get Your Child to Appreciate Good Food

What's wrong with chicken nuggets, anyway? Well, nothing at all that isn't wrong with any other kids' processed meat product formed from a sludge of mechanically-recovered meat, bulked out and bonded with additives, and enclosed in a fatty coating. What a sad substitute for real chicken.

These products may appear cheap, but it's a false economy because what you think you're buying (i.e. chicken, meat or fish) is padded out with cheap ingredients such as modified starch and fat. If money's tight, it's far better to buy a small amount of real meat or poultry and pad it out yourself with cheaper (but equally real) ingredients like beans or lentils (see 'Eating Better on a Budget', page 21). That way you'll be giving your child all the beneficial nutrients that come with those

pulses instead of the empty calories from modified starch (e.g. E1450 – starch sodium octenyl succinate).

> ***Top Tip:*** *Processed meat products can be a false economy; it's better to eke out real meat with beans and lentils.*

And, of course, so much of the fat in processed products – savoury or sweet – is of a very unfriendly nature: saturated fats and trans fats (as in 'hydrogenated vegetable oil') are bad news for your child's heart and arteries. Remember that the fatty deposits which cause heart disease are already forming in the arteries of pre-school children.

Not surprisingly, the taste of food residues held together by emulsifiers, stabilisers, thickeners, gelling agents, bulking agents

Process of Elimination

Food processing is not new. You can read about cheese in the Bible (2 Samuel 17:29, if you're interested). It's an ancient but effective way of preserving the protein, calcium and energy in milk. And today we would be lost without food processing which makes a wide variety of foods safe and available whenever we need them.

But not all processing is so helpful. Turning whole grains into white flour is a process of elimination – getting rid of useful nutrients and fibre. Not only does overprocessed food have some of the goodness removed: all too often, unhelpful ingredients such as fat, salt and sugar are added. You're probably glad you can buy chickens without feathers, heads and guts; but turning them into nuggets is a process too far.

and firming agents cannot compare with real food. But food manufacturers have an answer to that: they have a host of flavourings available to them and, as long as they add enough salt or sugar or both, the average palate will generally be satisfied.

And you soon learn to prefer something simply because it's familiar. Tastes and food preferences are habits. If you always have tea with sugar, it tastes wrong without it – at first. So if you feed your child salty or sugary food most of the time, you shouldn't be surprised when more natural, untainted food is rejected. Childhood is a unique period of learning. It's far easier to learn good habits in the first place than it is to unlearn bad ones.

Many children today exist on a diet of highly processed fast foods which are laden with saturated fat, salt, sugar and additives. Like Sam (see page 1), some are stuck with a restricted, unbalanced range of products. Not only are they heading for diabetes, high blood pressure and heart disease, but they remain pitifully unchallenged and uneducated – like a child who reads nothing but Noddy. There's an exciting world of literature beyond Noddy and Big-Ears; there's a wonderful world of food beyond nuggets and burgers.

But What Can I Do If My Child Just Wants Junk?

You know the one about the man who was asked for directions to a nearby village and replied, 'Now if I were you, to get *there*, I wouldn't start from here'? It might be tempting to give a similar answer to someone with an eleven-year-old who eats nothing but junk – on the basis that if you start in infancy, you can prevent such problems. But, of course, it would be equally absurd and unhelpful: wherever you want to go, you must start from where you are now.

It's true that if your child is still a baby, *now* is the time to take action. By introducing a wide variety of foods from six months, involving your baby in family meals and following the tips on pages 93–4, you can avoid getting caught in the 'kids' food trap'. But if your child is already a hardened junk food junkie, don't despair.

 Top Tip: *Even if your child is a hardened junk food junkie, don't give up!*

Hopeless?

When Laura was eight, her mother brought her to see me at the surgery. Perhaps it was my diagnostic sixth sense, or perhaps it was the way Laura coughed and spluttered her way to my desk, but I knew at once she had a cold. Laura's mother, Mandy, was a sensible woman and not someone who would normally bother the doctor about a cold. The trouble was, Laura seemed to have had nothing but colds in the previous six months; no sooner had she finished one, Mandy explained, than she started another. And she looked so pale all the time.

To cut a long consultation short, it became clear that Laura had a dismal diet. Apart from the chips, which always had to accompany the fatty fast food of the day, vegetables were vetoed. She even refused fruit other than a very occasional banana. She took a packed lunch to school and would generally have the crisps, the chocolate bar and the cola but, more often than not, brought anything else back home again.

When she came in from school, she was tired and hungry and was allowed to eat her evening meal in front of the TV. Her twelve-year-old twin brothers, Luke and Paul, got home from school later, on a school bus; they usually kicked a football around while Mandy prepared a separate meal for them. It wasn't until all the children had gone to bed that Mandy thought about getting herself something to eat. Another of her evening chores was to prepare Laura's packed lunch for the next day, knowing that some of it wouldn't be eaten.

Not that Mandy was happy about Laura's eating habits. On the contrary, but she didn't see how she could change things, as Laura was so set in her ways.

A way forward

We drew up a plan of action. Laura agreed that she wanted to learn a more grown-up way of eating, and the scheme was based on a loose contract between Laura and her mum to which

149

I acted as a witness. Laura was invited to name a number of foods which she would not be expected to eat (such as broad beans and spinach) but it still left a wealth of foods, including plenty of fruits and vegetables, which could be used.

We agreed that, with a little organisation, it was quite possible for the whole family to eat together at weekends and on most evenings of the week. This was an important part of the plan. During the week, Laura was to do her homework when she got in from school – before turning on the TV. She would have the same evening meal as the others, at the table, with the TV off. Eating her meal a bit later was no problem because she had a milkshake after school (made with banana or strawberries and skimmed milk in the food processor). She was also eating a better packed lunch which she helped Mandy to prepare (see Table 8).

To make this new routine more attractive to the children, Mandy would play a game with them after their evening meal together. Also, Laura's mealtime behaviour was included on a new reward chart. At the end of each day, Laura was allowed to stick coloured spots on a chart which listed twenty achievements such as 'I hung up my clothes neatly', 'I did my piano practice' and 'I ate my dinner well'. Mandy would award the mealtime marks if Laura ate and behaved well; she didn't necessarily have to clear the plate. At the end of each week, Laura's pocket money was based on her score. There were extra rewards for getting maximum points.

Mandy was surprised to find that she quite enjoyed the challenge of depending less on overprocessed convenience foods. She didn't have hours to spend in the kitchen, but she soon built up a repertoire of wholesome 'fast foods' – from beans on toast to stir-fried chicken and vegetables – acceptable to the whole family.

Table 8

Five Ways to Fill a Lunch Box

It's Monday morning and you suddenly realise you've forgotten the packed lunch (again). Here's a school-week's worth of ideas to inspire you. There are, of course, endless variations; just keep the four important food groups in mind. Always include a plastic drinking bottle of water. Always wash fruit (including clementines, etc., or dirt on the peel will be transferred to fingers and food).

1. Sandwich: wholegrain bread with olive-oil spread filled with tuna, yoghurt and sweetcorn
   Carrot sticks
   Lump of Cheddar cheese
   Apple
   Small tub of walnut pieces with raisins

2. Wholemeal pitta bread filled with Waldorf-type salad (e.g. chopped lettuce, apples, celery and walnuts, with raisins and mayonnaise or Greek yoghurt)
   Chicken drumstick
   Banana
   Home-made flapjack (see recipe page 187)

3. Breadsticks and sticks of vegetables (e.g. celery, cucumber, carrot, pepper) with a tasty dip such as hummus or cream cheese
   Salmon and salad in a bread roll
   Grapes
   Fruit yoghurt

4. Tub of pasta salad (e.g. cooked pasta, tuna, chopped celery, carrot and spring onion, with a mixture of mayonnaise and yoghurt)
   Small tub of cheese and pineapple chunks
   Pear
   Muesli bar

5. Wholemeal bread and peanut butter sandwich
   Tub of mixed bean salad
   Lump of soya cheese
   Peach or clementine
   Carrot cake

Stir-fried vegetables were a big hit with Laura (and so were chopsticks) so Mandy was delighted to discover packs of prepared vegetables in the supermarket. These provided a good assortment of ready-to-use, washed, cut vegetables – honest convenience food! Mandy also discovered that putting genuine chicken or fish under the grill wasn't so much less convenient than using chicken nuggets or fish fingers.

Miraculous transformation?

It wasn't that Laura changed from faddy child to grown-up gourmet overnight. At first, she would often leave some of the best things on her plate, but she soon learnt that they weren't going to be replaced with biscuits or crisps when she felt hungry. In fact, part of the new deal was that Mandy wouldn't keep any food in the house that she wasn't really happy for Laura to eat. But she did leave easy-to-reach, prepared vegetables such as carrot sticks in the fridge.

The new regime meant that Mandy was eating much better herself. She was delighted that, for the first time in ages, she had no trouble controlling her weight.

Laura needed to learn more about food. I encouraged Mandy to play food games with her. They started off with a simple food-tasting game: Laura would be given small samples of food to identify while wearing a blindfold.

 Top Tip: *If your child has a poor diet, increasing fruit and vegetable intake will make a big difference.*

When the whole family was together, Laura particularly enjoyed playing a game we made up. It was rather like *Pit* – you know, the card game in which you have a period of frantic 'trading' until someone wins by collecting all the barley or wheat or whatever. (I remember our neighbours saying, when I was a boy, how they always enjoyed hearing us play *Pit*!) Well, in this game, instead of different types of grain, each card showed a particular food such as cheese or carrots; to win, you had to collect all the cards belonging to one of the five food groups. Of course, Laura soon learnt about food groups and how to make up a balanced meal.

'Restaurants' was another of Laura's favourite games – especially when they played at mealtimes using real food. Sometimes she would be the waitress and take orders in her notebook; sometimes she was the customer in a posh restaurant with candles on the table. From time to time, Luke was the waiter, and Paul made a passable chef – as long as you ordered omelette.

This gave Mandy the confidence to take the children to a

reasonable restaurant – and it was a success! They hadn't been to a restaurant (just fast food outlets) since the time Laura smothered her spaghetti Bolognese in tomato ketchup – and left it all.

Children are more interested in eating food when they've had a hand in its preparation (but do make sure it's a clean hand). At weekends, Mandy started making time for Laura to 'help' with the cooking. These days, it's not uncommon for children to leave home before they acquire any kitchen skills (even opening a can of baked beans!).

Mandy was also able to involve Laura in the shopping. With an older child in a good mood (and that means being fed before a shopping expedition), this is a useful time to discuss such things as healthy choices, food safety and 'Use by' dates. (With younger children, the priority is to get to the checkout before *they* go bad.)

Gradually, Laura's attitude changed. She started to make friends with good food. Little by little, the range of foods she enjoyed increased. Five months on, I asked Mandy to make a note of everything Laura had to eat and drink for one week, and we compared this with Laura's dietary diary before the new 'contract'. Table 9 shows the main changes.

If At First You Don't Succeed . . .

Mandy reflected that, in the past, she had given up too easily. Laura had said she didn't like carrots or broccoli, so there seemed no point in serving them. It turned out that she disliked soft carrots and broccoli, but when they were lightly stir-fried and still crisp, it was another matter. Laura also liked roasted vegetables (see page 185). Mandy learnt the importance of

Table 9

Five months after a new 'contract', Laura was eating:	
More	**Less**
Fruit and vegetables	Fizzy drinks and sweets
Wholegrain pasta, bread, rice and cereals	
Jacket potatoes and new potatoes	Chips and crisps
Peas, beans, lentils and nuts	
Unprocessed fish, chicken and lean meat	Processed meat, e.g. burgers and nuggets
Skimmed milk and low-fat dairy products	
Home-made flapjack and fruit cake	Manufactured cakes, biscuits and puddings

trying rejected foods again, in a different form, after a decent interval.

 Top Tip: Ask your child to chop some vegetables for a stir-fry; some will get eaten before they reach the wok.

Laura was certainly eating better and, yes, she did have fewer colds. She also seemed happier, and her behaviour had improved; perhaps the reward chart and the extra attention at mealtimes had helped. They were doing more things together as a family. And now they could even go to a restaurant without hearing the words, 'Chicken nuggets and chips, please, Mum!'

Ten Ways to Help Your Child Appreciate Good Food

1. Eat together as a family as often as you can. Sit at the table and have the TV off.

2. Introduce a wide variety of foods from an early age – especially between six and nine months. Don't rely on highly processed convenience foods. Use foods in their natural, unprocessed state as much as possible. (Some processing is useful and some not: you want to eat whole grains but not whole chickens.)

3. Set a good example. Eat well; avoid fatty fast food; let your child see your enthusiasm for good food.

4. Keep wholesome snacks within easy reach (e.g. washed fruit, prepared vegetables like cucumber or celery sticks). Don't keep unhelpful foods (such as crisps and cream cakes) in the house (or in the shed for that matter); just don't buy them and the family won't eat them.

5. Serve food in an attractive way. It's true that broccoli and sweetcorn don't taste any different just because you arrange them like trees and haystacks – but it doesn't help if a meal looks like a compost heap.

6. Get the texture right. Children can be very sensitive to this. They may pronounce vegetables 'disgusting' when well cooked but enjoy them raw and crunchy or lightly stir-fried. Roasted vegetables are worth trying too. On the other hand, it may be necessary to cook, crush and sieve that veg beyond recognition – in a soup or spaghetti sauce, for example. Children are often suspicious of lumps lurking in liquid; a blender can make things go more smoothly.

7. Have fun with food. Never make eating a chore or have

fights over food. Play food games (such as food tastings to educate young palates, or games to teach about food groups). Reward good mealtime behaviour, but don't encourage bad behaviour by giving it attention.

8. Flaunt forbidden fruit. When Serena and Christabel were younger, they enjoyed 'stealing' pieces of chopped fruit from our plates. So we made a game of this – pretending to be dismayed that yet another piece was missing when we looked down at the plate. They'd eat far more fruit that way than if we gave them a little plate of their own fruit. Now 'family fruit' has become a tradition: I prepare a platter of assorted sliced fruit and put it in the middle of the table after the first course; we all have our own fork and dive in.

9. Let your child loose in the kitchen – under close supervision! When children help to choose and prepare food, they are more likely to eat it (even if it does put the adults off). In any case, they need to learn about buying, storing and preparing food.

10. Find out which of your child's friends have healthy appetites for good food and invite them round for meals. Your child may follow their example.

'Help! My Child's Turned into a Teenager'

How to Cope When the Hormones Kick In

'Ah, Dan,' sighed Carol, catching sight of her son's scruffy silhouette in the kitchen doorway. 'What time do you call this?'

Dan grunted.

'Your porridge is getting cold,' continued Carol, reaching for another piece of toast. Carol contemplated the irony that such a short while ago Dan would jump out of bed at the crack of dawn, waking them all up, but now he was fourteen they needed a winch to get him up in time.

Dan squinted towards the kitchen table where his parents and sixteen-year-old sister, Louise, were having breakfast. He grunted, yawned, scratched his head and shuffled towards the fridge.

'You'd better get a move on,' said Carol, pushing the bowl

of porridge further towards Dan's usual place at the table.

'Eh?' groaned Dan.

'Your porridge,' answered Carol, gesturing towards the bowl's not-so-steamy, solidifying contents. 'I can heat it in the microwave for you, if you like.'

'Oh, don't hassle me, Mum. You know I don't have time for breakfast,' moaned Dan – revealing, uncharacteristically, that he could speak fluent English.

'Well, you would have time if you got up earlier,' said Carol.

'Not much chance of that, under the circumstances, eh Dan?' taunted Louise.

'Shut up!' whined Dan, aware that his big sister was threatening to let it slip that he'd smuggled four bottles of beer into his room last night. This was strictly against the house rules.

'Don't like breakfast,' he mumbled, hoping to divert attention from Louise's bait.

'It's not healthy to miss breakfast, is it, Dad?' said Carol.

'That's right,' agreed Geoff, emitting a cloud of smoke from behind his newspaper.

'Not that you'll waste away,' continued Carol in Dan's direction. 'Dad and I only had four chips between us last night. And two of those were burnt. I've never seen anyone put away so much. You must have hollow legs.'

'He's got weedy legs, haven't you, Dan?' said Louise. 'But he's hoping to transform himself into Arnold Schwarzenegger's double by next week.'

'I'm not,' said Dan, looking embarrassed and sticking his head in the fridge.

'We found the evidence,' continued Louise. 'There are body building magazines in your room . . .'

'You've no business to –'

'*And* ... cartons of Liquid Protein Formula for Body Builders!' shouted Louise, triumphantly.

'Well at least I'm not on a permanent diet,' said a muffled voice from the fridge.

'That's true, Louise,' said Carol. 'You've only had two bites of toast. You're getting too skinny lately.'

Dan seemed to have found what he was looking for. Dropping two cans of cola and a chocolate bar into his bag, he slammed the fridge door, grunted and started to walk out.

'You can't go off to school without any breakfast,' said Carol.

Dan grunted and carried on towards the front door. Then, suddenly remembering something, he stopped in his tracks and returned to the kitchen.

'Dad, got five quid for the chippy later?' he asked, briefly finding his vocabulary again.

Geoff reached into his pocket, and a banknote appeared from behind his paper. Dan took the note, grunted and set off for school.

Top Tip: *Your teenager may seem to have lost the power of speech and the sense to eat properly. It's not permanent.*

Metamorphosis

It's almost magical when the process of metamorphosis transforms an ugly, inexpressive caterpillar into a delightful butterfly. And when you wake up to find your affectionate, talkative child has turned into a teenager, it's much the same – but in reverse!

In fact, of course, the teenage years are a time of transition

161

"HE WAS ALRIGHT WHEN HE WENT TO BED."

('pupation' if you like) from childhood to adulthood. No doubt, Carol found trying to get a response out of Dan as he lay immobile in his bed was about as productive as prodding an insect pupa. And sometimes things weren't much better when he was up.

Teenagers are desperate to assert their independence, and to conform within their peer group; at the same time they are struggling with emotional turmoil and bewildering changes in their bodies. All this has an influence on eating behaviour during adolescence.

Here are ten teenage traits you are likely to run into which can all have significant effects both on nutrition and on parental sanity:

1. *Missing breakfast*

Many teenagers, like Dan, will set off for school without breakfast. This may not be nutritionally ideal, but they make up for it one way or another. If you can get your

162

teenager to take a banana, so much the better – especially if it doesn't return black and squashed in the bottom of the school bag.

2. Snacking

No doubt Dan's chocolate and cola would not be the only snack of the day; teenagers tend to boost their diets with confectionery and crisps. Although these foods have their faults (e.g. empty sugar calories, excess salt), they do also supply some nutrients (e.g. calcium from chocolate, potassium from crisps). If you provide a healthy, balanced menu at home, these snacks, for all their faults, aren't worth worrying about during the teenage years.

3. Experimenting with alcohol

Dan's bottles of beer in the bedroom might seem harmless enough, but he is entering a real danger zone. Where will it end? Alcohol-related accidents are the commonest cause of death in the 15–24 age group. Parental prohibition may lead to dangerous rebellion. The best approach is to encourage a responsible attitude from the earliest days by setting a good example – sometimes enjoying a little alcohol at mealtimes, but not if driving. The teenager who is allowed some alcohol during family meals is less likely to go wild at other times.

 Top Tip: *Many teenage traits are harmless, but experimenting with alcohol is a danger zone.*

4. ### Knocking back the cola
    Teenagers often consume large quantities of fizzy soft drinks. Far rather lemonade than lager, of course, but these drinks are packed with empty sugar calories and are a dentist's delight (assuming the dentist is paid a fee for every filling and extraction).

5. ### Filling up on fast food
    As cars top up at filling stations, so today's teenagers stop off at fast food outlets to refuel. Like it or not, unless your teenager is unusual, 'junk' food will make a significant contribution to nutrition.

6. ### Eating you out of house and home
    Evidently, Carol hadn't allowed enough food for Dan's voracious appetite the previous evening. Feeding frenzies of this sort are common at certain stages of development (typically around the age of twelve for a girl and fourteen for a boy). A teenaged boy might put away as many as 4000 Kcal a day without getting fat. Don't try that as an adult!

7. ### Dieting
    Like Louise, a lot of teenaged girls are on diets. If they want any guidance on how to go about it, there's no shortage of daft diets to choose from. Girls who adopt very restricted diets consisting of only one or two items (such as black coffee and fruit, or cabbage soup) are clearly

heading for nutritional deficiency (but at least with a cabbage soup diet, the ferocious flatulence will soon blast them back to reality!).

Dabbling with diets is normal, but it is important to recognise when something more sinister is developing. The eating disorders anorexia nervosa and bulimia nervosa are very serious conditions, but the sooner they are recognised the better. Referral, ideally to a team including a psychiatrist and dietitian, can be life-saving. Features to look out for are: preoccupation with food; fear of gaining weight despite being underweight; feeling fat when actually thin; binge eating followed by vomiting; use of laxatives or diuretics to control weight. If you have any cause for concern, discuss it with your doctor.

Top Tip: *Most teenaged girls go on diets, but watch out for early signs of an eating disorder.*

8. Going vegetarian

Whether it's a TV programme about abattoirs, contact with an animal welfare group, or a dissection in school biology, something triggers a lot of teenagers to turn vegetarian. Often this is only a phase.

A vegetarian diet can be very healthy, but teenagers often don't understand that there's more to it than simply cutting out animal products.

As a parent, you are unlikely to gain much by aggressively arguing that pigs have nothing better to do than be eaten. It's usually more helpful to provide support and sound information (see pages 51–7). Teenagers who exclude animal products without reliable information risk deficiency of iron, zinc, protein, calcium and vitamin B_{12}. (Anaemia is quite common in teenaged girls who need plenty of iron to make up for the blood lost at each period.) Let them come back to the bacon butties when and if they choose.

9. Body building

It's quite normal for young people to have worries about their changing bodies. Is this bit too fat? Is that bit too short? Just as girls are often obsessed with losing weight, so boys, like Dan, often crave bigger and better muscles. They may spend hours in the gym, striving for a six-pack they've seen on the big screen. From time to time I see teenaged boys in my surgery with injuries caused by weight training. It's not uncommon to find that they are taking bizarre supplements (not to mention anabolic steroids) or have made inappropriate dietary changes in the hope of boosting the growth of bulging muscles.

10. Worrying about spots

Nobody wants acne and, understandably, this is a serious worry for some teenagers. So what effect does diet have on acne? Is it all down to the sweets, chocolates and deep-fried food? No.

There have been experiments which have failed to show, for example, that chocolate makes a difference. So it would be quite wrong to tell a young person with severe acne that a good diet will solve the problem. Mind you, some people go to the other extreme and say that diet makes no difference at all. That's squeezing a dogma out of rather scrappy evidence (a bit like an astronaut suggesting he'd disproved the existence of God because he didn't bump into him on the way to the moon).

A good diet will benefit your teenager in lots of ways and is likely to help the skin – even though acne won't disappear overnight. In particular, it's worth suggesting: plenty of fruit and vegetables (including carrots for vitamin A); less saturated fat (e.g. from processed meat products) and more friendly fats (e.g. from nuts, seeds and unsaturated oils); good sources of zinc (e.g. lean meat, shellfish and wholemeal bread). If concern about the skin leads to a much better diet, that can only be a good thing.

But if your teenager has a significant problem with acne, it's well worth a visit to the doctor. There are treatments that make a real difference – but you have to keep going for some weeks before you start to see the results.

How Can I Help My Teenager?

The first thing is to relax. Grunting, ignoring everything you say, and snacking on any old junk, although characteristic of pigs, are also normal facets of teenage behaviour. We've all been there. The survival rate is very high. Although some would never admit to it, even the most inspiring adults were teenagers once.

Secondly, don't have unnecessary battles. How serious is it that your daughter misses breakfast – when she'll be tucking

BUT MUM I DON'T EAT BREAKFAST!

CEREAL

DON'T HAVE UNNECESSARY BATTLES.

into a yoghurt and banana at 11 o'clock if hunger strikes? Does it really matter if your teenager stops eating meat for a while (as long as high quality protein is supplied by pulses and grains)? Don't alienate your teenager by fighting over trivia: it will only incite more extreme behaviour and reduce your impact on things that really count.

 Top Tip: *Don't fight over trivia; draw a firm line where it really matters. Support and information achieve more than opposition.*

Draw a firm, clear line where it really matters. For example, don't be vague and laid-back about drinking and driving. Your teenager can respect firm limits if you don't try to impose unnecessary restrictions.

Of course, with all the big issues – such as attitudes to drink,

168

drugs, smoking, and sex – it's a bit late to confront the matter for the first time when your child has a problem. There's no substitute for a firm foundation in childhood before the pressures of puberty start clouding communications. Discussing these things with your child over the years – quite naturally as questions arise – helps to build defences against the onslaught of peer group pressure later on. It's not just your *words*, of course, that carry weight during those years when your wisdom goes unchallenged: it's the way you live as well. If your child sees you drunk, your words about responsible drinking will have a hollow ring.

The foundations laid in childhood must go deeper still. Children develop self-esteem as they experience their parents' unconditional love throughout the childhood years, confirming their unique value and boosting their confidence. (See *The Parentalk Guide to the Childhood Years* by Steve Chalke published by Hodder & Stoughton.) It is this inner strength – much more than rules and regulations – that can protect your child from coming a cropper in the teenage years. So many teenage tragedies have their roots in low self-esteem. In a nutshell: you will do far more to protect your daughter against an eating disorder by demonstrating unconditional love – from her earliest days – than by insisting that she eats her dinner.

 Top Tip: *The foundations you lay early on will help your child to weather the storms of the teenage years.*

A Tall Order

Yes, parenthood is a daunting responsibility, isn't it? Don't worry. There's no such thing as a perfect parent, but there are lots of highly successful parents and you can be one too. It's not being flawless that counts. The important thing is to send your child this message: 'I love you and, simply because you're you, I will always love you – whether you succeed or fail.' The child who really understands that message can ride the turbulence of the teenage years.

So, don't despair. Faced with your grunting, grazing teenager, you may feel years of effort to feed your child a balanced diet have gone to waste. They haven't.

Not only have you got your child off to a good start, but you also have more influence than you think. After all, you choose what foods and drinks to buy and store in your cupboards and your fridge. This is what your teenager will eat and drink at home – whether in family meals or midnight raids on the fridge. No doubt, it will sometimes be supplemented by fast foods and confectionery. That's inevitable.

But after the temporary turmoil of these years, the firm foundation you have laid for your child will still be there, guiding behaviour in matters of food and drink – and in the rest of life.

Family Recipes

Eating together is one of the pillars on which family life is built. Here are some recipes that adults and children can enjoy together.

And the Baby?

It's a good idea to include your baby in the family meal from six to nine months – even if you do have to chop, mash or even liquidise some dishes. Of course, there may be certain ingredients, such as nut products, that you will want to avoid giving your child until later on if you have a family history of allergy. Don't give whole nuts to children under five because of the risk of choking.

Salt

You will notice that there is no added salt in these recipes. It's essential not to add salt to a baby's food and it's far better for the whole family to get used to low-salt cuisine. The palate soon adjusts. If older family members are already in the habit of eating highly salted food, it's sensible to reduce the addition of salt *gradually* to avoid protests. If you want to add salt, use LoSalt or Solo which have a reduced sodium content.

Stock

Most commercial stock products have a high salt content. When it's not convenient to make your own stock, use a product such as *low-salt* vegetable bouillon powder, or one of the low-salt, ready-made refrigerated stocks that simply need to be diluted.

Eggs

Eggs often have a bad name among the health conscious because of the fat and cholesterol content of the yolk. One option is to use two egg whites for every whole egg suggested by the recipe. Alternatively, you could use Columbus eggs which contain more of the beneficial omega-3 (n-3) fatty acids than standard eggs. Mind you, no matter how friendly the fat content, as sure as eggs is eggs, the yolk will still contain a fair dose of cholesterol. You needn't bother about this when a recipe uses one egg between four people, but it can mount up when one person has whole eggs; standard advice is to have no more than three egg yolks a week.

Quantities

These recipes 'serve 4', although this doesn't always mean just four single portions (e.g. the fruit cake, pages 188–9). If you have a huge family, it's easy enough to double the quantities. If there are only two of you, it's often worth making more than you can eat and putting some in the freezer.

Spoon measures are level; tsp = teaspoon; tbsp = tablespoon.

oOo

Turkey Burgers

Most children like burgers. Sadly, so many burgers are packed with poor-quality ingredients. These turkey burgers are full of goodness instead of saturated fat, salt and additives. Our girls love them.

450 g (1 lb) extra lean turkey mince
2 slices wholemeal bread (for breadcrumbs)
1 small onion, peeled and chopped
1 tomato, chopped
1 apple, chopped (no need to peel)
1 medium carrot, peeled and chopped
1 egg, beaten
30 ml (2 tbsp) finely chopped parsley
5 ml (1 tsp) dried mixed herbs
5 ml (1 tsp) cayenne pepper
2.5 ml (½ tsp) cumin
rapeseed oil for shallow frying

Put the turkey mince in a large mixing bowl. Cut the bread into chunks and convert to breadcrumbs in a food processor; put the breadcrumbs to one side. Process the onion, tomato, apple and carrot together in the food processor and add to the turkey mince. Mix in the beaten egg, parsley, herbs and spices, adding breadcrumbs until the mixture is stodgy enough to hold its shape. Use very clean hands rather than a spoon for this stage to avoid beating all the texture out of the meat.

Form the mixture into about 10 burgers (8–12, depending on size) on a floured board and chill in the fridge for at least an hour before cooking (chill the burgers, I mean, not yourself). The burgers can be frozen at this stage and defrosted in the fridge before cooking. To shallow fry, heat a minimum of rapeseed oil in a heavy-bottomed pan and cook the burgers for about 15 minutes, turning twice, to make sure they're cooked right through. Alternatively, they can be brushed with oil and grilled or barbecued. Serve with ketchup or low-fat mayonnaise, burger buns and lettuce.

Cock, Stock and Barrel

You don't need a whole barrel of cider to make this delicious family meal. All it takes is half a kilo of chicken, half a pint of stock and half a pint of cider – as well as the vegetables, of course. This dish will go down just as well at a dinner party as in the nursery.

It may seem a bit rum to put alcohol in recipes for children. I certainly wouldn't recommend sherry trifle, but in recipes like this one the alcohol is removed by cooking. If you want to leave out the cider, just cook 'cock in stock'.

15 ml (1 tbsp) olive or rapeseed oil
4 skinless, boneless chicken breasts, cut into chunks
2 rashers of lean, smoked bacon, chopped
1 medium onion, finely chopped
1 garlic clove, crushed
45 ml (3 tbsp) plain flour
300 ml (½ pt) stock (e.g. *low-salt* vegetable bouillon)
300 ml (½ pt) dry cider
2 celery sticks, chopped
2 carrots, chopped
2 courgettes, chopped
100 g (4 oz) button mushrooms, halved
5 ml (1 tsp) dried mixed herbs

Heat the oil in a large pan and fry the chicken and bacon for about 5 minutes, stirring, until the chicken chunks are sealed all over. Using a slotted spoon, remove the chicken and bacon from the pan and transfer to a casserole. Fry the onion in the remaining oil for about 3 minutes, then add the garlic and stir while the garlic softens. Still stirring, sprinkle in the flour.

Gradually add the stock, stirring, and then the cider. Bring to the boil and add the remaining ingredients. Simmer for 5 minutes and mix with the chicken in the casserole. Cover and cook in a preheated oven at 180 °C (350 °F, gas 4) for 1 hour. Serve with rice or potatoes.

Stir-fried Chicken and Vegetables

Children who wouldn't look twice at limp cabbage often enjoy stir-fried vegetables – and trying to eat them with chopsticks. The combination with chicken is lovely. Tofu works well too, especially if an interesting marinade or sauce is used. It's important to cut the vegetables into small pieces – bags of prepared vegetables are extremely convenient.

15 ml (1 tbsp) rapeseed oil
4 skinless, boneless chicken breasts, cut into strips
1 garlic clove, finely chopped
25 g (1 oz) root ginger, peeled and finely chopped
1 carrot, peeled and cut into thin batons
100 g (4 oz) red and yellow peppers, cut into strips
75 g (3 oz) broccoli, cut into small florets
75 g (3 oz) savoy cabbage, shredded
75 g (3 oz) beansprouts
75 g (3 oz) mangetout, topped, tailed and halved
75 g (3 oz) baby sweetcorn, halved
50 g (2 oz) button mushrooms, sliced

4 spring onions, finely chopped
black pepper

With the wok (or large saucepan) over a high heat, get the oil really hot before adding the chicken. Fry the chicken for a few minutes (without stirring it) until browned and cooked right through. Add the garlic and ginger, and stir-fry for about 1 minute; add the remaining ingredients. Continue to stir briskly for another 4–5 minutes but serve before the vegetables lose their enthusiasm.

Fish Casserole

This nutritious family meal is easy to prepare, particularly if you buy the fish ready to use with skin and bones removed. You can turn it into 'tipsy fish casserole' by adding cider or wine, but make sure the alcohol is added at the beginning of the cooking time – and not at the end – or you'll have a tipsy child!

700 g (1½ lb) white fish fillets (e.g. cod, haddock or coley)
juice of 1 lemon
15 ml (1 tbsp) olive oil
1 onion, peeled and chopped
1 garlic clove, crushed
400 g (14 oz) can chopped tomatoes
1 green pepper, deseeded and chopped
100 g (4 oz) button mushrooms, halved
30 ml (2 tbsp) chopped fresh parsley
5 ml (1 tsp) dried mixed herbs
75 g (3 oz) cheese, grated
75 g (3 oz) wholemeal breadcrumbs

Wash the fish fillets, remove any skin or bones, and cut into bite-sized cubes. Place the fish in an ovenproof casserole and sprinkle it with the lemon juice. Heat the oil in a pan and sauté the onion for a few minutes before adding the garlic. Once the onion and garlic are soft, add the tomatoes, pepper, mushrooms, parsley and herbs. Simmer for 5 minutes, then pour the sauce over the fish. Cover the casserole and bake in the oven at 160 °C (325 °F, gas 3) for 30 minutes.

Remove the lid and sprinkle the cheese and breadcrumbs over the casserole before returning it to the oven for about 15 minutes or browning the top under the grill.

Fish Cakes

Home-made fish cakes can be a wholesome convenience food if you knock them up when you have time and keep some in the freezer. They're delicious with parsley sauce (see page 178).

This recipe starts from scratch, but you can use leftover mashed potatoes and any cooked fish (in roughly equal quantities). It also works well with tinned salmon.

225 g (½ lb) fish, e.g. cod, haddock or salmon
450 g (1 lb) potatoes, peeled and quartered
1 egg, beaten
45 ml (3 tbsp) chopped parsley
45 ml (3 tbsp) chopped chives
black pepper
45 ml (3 tbsp) wholemeal flour

Put the washed fish in a pan and add skimmed milk until the fish is just covered. Place a lid on the pan and bring slowly to the boil; simmer gently for 5 minutes, turn off the heat and leave the fish in the covered pan for another 5 minutes. Pour off the liquid and use this to make parsley sauce. Remove the skin and flake the fish, taking great care to get rid of any bones.

Boil the potatoes for 20 minutes, or until soft, and mash. Mix the potatoes and fish in a large bowl, adding the egg, parsley, chives and black pepper. Form the mixture into 8 cakes and roll each one in wholemeal flour.

Chill the fish cakes in the fridge for an hour before cooking. Alternatively, freeze them (on a tray before storing in the freezer in a sealed container) and defrost in the fridge before cooking. They can be fried (in a little olive or rapeseed oil) grilled or baked. Serve with tomatoes, peas and parsley sauce (and you'll have the four important food groups on a plate).

Parsley Sauce

This is an ideal accompaniment for fish cakes or fish. Traditionally, white sauce is made with a roux (fat and flour paste), but you can make a very low-fat sauce using cornflour and skimmed milk. If the skimmed milk is first used to poach the fish, so much the better.

25 ml (1½ tbsp) cornflour
300 ml (½ pint) skimmed milk
30 ml (2 tbsp) chopped parsley
pepper

Put the cornflour in a cold saucepan and blend with 15–30ml (1–2 tbsp) of the milk until smooth. Slowly add the remaining milk, off the heat, stirring to prevent lumps forming. Gently heat the cold mixture, stirring continuously, until the sauce boils. Cook gently for 2–3 minutes, then stir in the parsley and pepper. Don't boil again unless you want a green sauce.

Crispy Cod Fingers

This is a real treat for our children and, unlike a lot of commercial products, these fish fingers are free of unwanted additives. Of course, you can use other fish such as coley and haddock (and you may have to if cod disappears from the North Sea). It's often convenient to use frozen fillets.

450 g (1 lb) boneless, skinless cod fillets
60 ml (4 tbsp) plain flour
1 egg, beaten
75 g (3 oz) wholemeal breadcrumbs
rapeseed oil for frying

Wash the fish under running cold water and dry on absorbent kitchen paper. Cut into 'fingers' (and I'm sure these taste better if they're not precisely rectangular). Cutting larger portions reduces the overall fat content of the meal once it is fried.

Arrange three shallow dishes side-by-side: one containing the flour, one the beaten egg, and the other the breadcrumbs. Coat each portion of fish first in flour, then egg, then breadcrumbs.

Heat a little rapeseed oil in a frying pan and shallow fry the fish for about 10 minutes, turning once, until golden brown all over. Serve with plenty of fresh lemon juice and peas.

Tuna and Pasta Bake

Pasta is often popular with children. It's also a great way to give your family carbohydrate because, with its low glycaemic index (see page 12), pasta releases its energy slowly. Unfortunately, a lot of pasta dishes are spoilt by fatty sauces swimming in saturates. Here's a healthy meal with a Mediterranean flavour.

1 onion, peeled and finely chopped
1 garlic clove, crushed
15 ml (1 tbsp) olive oil
1 red pepper, deseeded and chopped
1 celery stick, finely chopped
1 courgette, chopped
15 ml (1 tbsp) tomato purée
400 g (14 oz) can chopped tomatoes
30 ml (2 tbsp) chopped fresh parsley
10 ml (2 tsp) dried mixed herbs
450 g (1 lb) pasta shells
400 g (14 oz) can tuna in water, drained
75 g (3 oz) cheese, grated
75 g (3 oz) wholemeal breadcrumbs

Sauté the onion in the oil for a few minutes before adding the garlic. As soon as the garlic has softened, add the other vegetables, tomato purée, tomatoes and herbs and simmer while cooking the pasta; cook the pasta in a separate pan of boiling water until *al dente* (still slightly firm).

Drain the pasta and mix it with the sauce and the flaked tuna fish in an ovenproof dish, e.g. 30 cm × 24 cm (12 in × 9½ in). Top this with the grated cheese and breadcrumbs. Bake in the oven at 190 °C (375 °F, gas 5) for 20 minutes or until the topping is crisp and golden brown. Serve with peas or salad.

Quick Pizza

You can have this simple snack on your table much faster than you can have a pizza delivered to your door – and you avoid unwanted ingredients. Of course, you can vary the toppings; this one includes the four important food groups. Whether you use Cheddar cheese or reduced-fat mozzarella (perhaps topped with a little grated Parmesan), the results are delicious.

    4 wholemeal pitta breads
    120 ml (8 tbsp) tomato sauce for pizza or pasta
    200 g (7 oz) can tuna in water, drained and flaked
    227 g (8 oz) can pineapple pieces, drained
    75 g (3 oz) cheese, grated or thinly sliced

Place the pittas on a tray and coat the upper surface of each one with tomato sauce. Top with tuna, pineapple and, finally, cheese. Place under a hot grill for 3–5 minutes. Eat with a knife and fork or cut into finger food for younger children.

Easy Peasy Dhal

Dhal, or lentil purée, is a traditional Indian dish that's easy to make and this version is certainly peasy: it's made with split peas. It's a hit in our house. You can always tone down (or step up!) the spices according to your child's palate. Many Asian children grow up eating spicy food from infancy. Of course, if you order dhal from the local Indian restaurant, it will probably be swimming in ghee. Here's all the goodness without the 'badness'.

    225 g (8 oz) yellow split peas
    2.5 ml (½ tsp) ground turmeric
    seeds of 1 cardamom, crushed
    10 ml (2 tsp) rapeseed oil
    5 ml (1 tsp) ground cumin
    5 ml (1 tsp) ground coriander
    2 garlic cloves, crushed

Wash the split peas and soak in plenty of cold water overnight; drain and rinse. Put the split peas in a pan with 900 ml (1½ pt) of water and bring to the boil. Remove any scum. Add the turmeric and cardamom, and simmer gently for 1 hour or until thoroughly mushy. As the dhal softens, turn the heat right down and stir to prevent it from sticking and burning.

Heat the oil in a separate pan, add the cumin and coriander, and cook for a few minutes before adding the garlic. Once the garlic is golden, mix the contents of this pan into the dhal. Serve hot or cold with pitta bread – or with chutneys, raita and curry!

Rolled Dhal

I don't know what the great children's author, Roald Dahl, would have made of these lentil rolls, but they're popular with some of his young readers (who might not otherwise eat lentils – a good source of protein and iron). There's no need to soak red lentils.

225 g (8 oz) split red lentils, washed
600 ml (1 pint) stock (e.g. *low-salt* vegetable bouillon)
1 onion, peeled and finely chopped
1 garlic clove, crushed
2.5 ml (½ tsp) ground cumin
2.5 ml (½ tsp) ground coriander
juice of ½ lemon
1 egg, beaten
60 ml (4 tbsp) wholemeal flour
rapeseed oil for frying

Put the lentils, stock, onion, garlic, and spices into a pan, bring to the boil and simmer gently for 30 minutes, or until the lentils are tender, stirring to avoid any burning while forming a thick paste. Remove from the heat and allow to cool (which you can speed up by standing the pan in cold water) before stirring in the lemon juice and egg.

Form the mixture into sausage-shaped portions of about 25 mm (1 in) diameter, finally rolling each one on a board coated in wholemeal flour. To freeze, place the rolls on an open tray in the freezer and pack in a sealed container once frozen. To cook, heat a little rapeseed oil in a heavy-bottomed pan, add the rolls and fry until golden brown on all sides. Serve in a roll like a hot dog, with chutney, ketchup or a slosh of HP Sauce which has the authentic brown colour of 'George's Marvellous Medicine'.

Bean Stew

This is a simple recipe using canned pulses and it only takes a few minutes to chuck all the ingredients in the pot. You can start with dry pulses, using only 400 g (14 oz), soaking them overnight, and extending the cooking time until they are soft. Beans provide valuable protein along with other nutrients and fibre. Not only will serving this stew give your family a nutritional boost, you can also enjoy the old joke with your children. (Man: 'Waiter, Waiter, what's this?' Waiter: 'It's bean stew, Sir.' Man: 'I don't care what it's *been*! What is it *now*?')

15 ml (1 tbsp) olive or rapeseed oil
1 onion, peeled and chopped
2 courgettes, chopped
100 g (4 oz) button mushrooms, halved
400 g (14 oz) can chopped tomatoes
15 ml (1 tbsp) tomato purée
410 g (14 oz) can beans (e.g. red kidney, blackeye, haricot, or
    mixed), drained and rinsed
410 g (14 oz) can chickpeas, drained and rinsed
15 ml (1 tbsp) chopped parsley
10 ml (2 tsp) dried mixed herbs
black pepper

Heat the oil in a heavy-bottomed saucepan and sauté the onion until soft. Add all the other ingredients, cover, bring to the boil and simmer gently for 30 minutes. Serve with rice or pasta.

Sneaky Soup

A lot of children are put off by lumps of vegetable matter lurking in soups and sauces. This delicious tomato-based soup sneaks in some extra vegetables but, because of its smooth texture, you would never know. If you want to use it as a pasta sauce, add a little less stock to make it thicker.

15 ml (1 tbsp) olive or rapeseed oil
1 medium onion, peeled and finely chopped
2 celery sticks, finely chopped
3 large carrots, peeled and finely chopped
1 red pepper, deseeded and finely chopped
1 garlic clove, crushed
700 g (1½ lb) thick, sieved tomatoes (e.g. passata or 'creamed' tomatoes)
900 ml (1½ pt) stock (e.g. *low-salt* vegetable bouillon)
100 g (4 oz) pasta (e.g. penne)
50 g (2 oz) cheese, grated

Heat the oil in a large saucepan and sauté the onion, celery, carrots and red pepper for about 5 minutes and then add the garlic. Sauté for 2–3 more minutes, stirring frequently, and add the sieved tomatoes. Use some of the stock to rinse the residual tomato from the container into the saucepan. Add the remaining stock, bring the soup to the boil and simmer for about 30 minutes, almost completely covered.

Remove the saucepan from the heat and allow to cool a little. Use a hand blender to liquidise the cooked vegetables until the soup is completely lump-free. (Alternatively, the soup can be transferred to a liquidiser in 2 or 3 batches.) Bring the soup back to the boil and add more water if it's too thick. Add the pasta and simmer for ten minutes, stirring occasionally. Serve, and sprinkle each portion with grated cheese.

Roast Vegetables

Children who reject soft or mushy vegetables often enjoy the firmness and flavour of roasted vegetables. Here is a colourful collection – not only delicious, but also bursting with antioxidants. Roasted root vegetables such as parsnips, turnips and carrots are lovely too.

    4 garlic cloves (optional)
    100 g (4 oz) mushrooms, wiped
    2 red onions, peeled
    2 large tomatoes
    2 peppers (one red, one yellow), deseeded
    2 courgettes
    1 aubergine
    1 fennel bulb
    15 ml (1 tbsp) olive or rapeseed oil
    black pepper

Leaving the garlic cloves and mushrooms whole, cut the vegetables into large chunks; halve the tomatoes; cut the fennel in half from top to bottom and slice each half. Arrange the vegetables in a large, lightly oiled ovenproof dish or roasting tin; brush them with a little oil and season with black pepper. Roast in a preheated oven at 220 °C (425 °F, gas 7) for about 25 minutes, turning after about 15 minutes.

Roast Potatoes

Traditional roast potatoes are soaked in saturated fat from lard or dripping. There's no need for this at all and you can cook perfect roast potatoes that will delight your family and do them a power of good.

> 6 potatoes (depending on the sizes of potatoes and appetites)
> 15 ml (1 tbsp) rapeseed oil

Peel the potatoes (or scrub them if you are leaving the skins on). Cut them into large chunks and boil for 10 minutes.

Meanwhile pour the oil in a roasting tin and heat in the oven at 220 °C (425 °F, gas 7). Drain the potatoes thoroughly and 'fluff' them a little by shaking them in the pan over a very low heat.

Transfer the potatoes to the hot roasting tin and, working quickly (preferably with the roasting tin over a low heat to keep the oil hot), turn them with tongs to ensure they are lightly coated with hot oil. Return the roasting tin to the oven and cook the potatoes (turning them a couple of times to keep them lightly coated with oil) for about 40 minutes until crisp and golden brown.

Oven Chips

Of course, you can buy oven chips and they'll be a lot less fatty than deep-fried ones. Cooking your own allows you to choose the oil and use very little of it. You also get a real potato taste, often lacking in frozen chips made from reconstituted potato.

> 3 large potatoes, peeled
> 15 ml (1 tbsp) rapeseed oil

Cut the potatoes into chips and boil them for just 2 or 3 minutes to avoid turning them soft. Drain off the water and dry the potato on absorbent kitchen paper. Pour the oil onto a baking tray and heat in the oven at 220 °C (425 °F, gas 7). Spread the chips on the tray, turning them over to make sure they are lightly coated with oil on all sides. Bake for about 40 minutes, turning a couple of times, until they are crisp and golden. If you want to serve with salt, use a little LoSalt or Solo.

Date and Walnut Flapjack

The nourishing oats in flapjack come with a good helping of fat and sugar. At least this version uses friendly fats, avoiding the saturated fat from butter in traditional recipes and the trans fats in manufactured products. It's delicious too – whether you add the dates and walnuts or not. You could even include some chocolate drops as a special treat.

45 ml (3 tbsp) golden syrup
100 g (4 oz) 'olive oil' reduced-fat spread (59 per cent fat)
225 g (8 oz) rolled oats
75 g (3 oz) pitted dates, chopped
75 g (3 oz) walnuts, chopped

Warm the syrup in a large saucepan and stir in the spread, then the oats, dates and walnuts.

Line the bottom of a straight-sided, shallow 18 cm (7 in) square tin with non-stick baking parchment. Transfer the mixture to the tin and press down well. Bake at 180 °C (350 °F, gas 4) for about 30 minutes, until golden brown. Cut into small squares while warm, but leave in the tin until cold.

Prune Purée

With some baked foods, you can replace the fat called for by the recipe with the same weight of prune purée. Fruit cake is an ideal example (see below). To prepare 280 g (10 oz) of prune purée, blend 225 g (8 oz) of ready-to-eat prunes with 90 ml (6 tbsp) water in a food processor to form a smooth paste.

Rich Fruit Cake

This is as delicious as any fruit cake and you would never guess it's made without added fat.

    280 g (10 oz) currants
    200 g (7 oz) sultanas
    110 g (4 oz) raisins
    70 g (2½ oz) glacé cherries, quartered
    70 g (2½ oz) almonds, chopped
    70 g (2½ oz) cut mixed peel
    grated rind of 1 lemon
    30 ml (2 tbsp) brandy
    200 g (7 oz) plain wholemeal flour
    5 ml (1 tsp) ground mixed spice
    2.5 ml (½ tsp) grated nutmeg
    60 g (2 oz) ground almonds
    175 g (6 oz) soft brown sugar
    175 g (6 oz) prune purée
    15 ml (1 tbsp) black treacle
    4 eggs, beaten (or 8 egg whites)

Mix the dried fruit, cherries, chopped almonds, peel, lemon rind and brandy in a bowl. (This mixture may be covered and left to stand overnight.)

Sift the flour, spice and nutmeg into another bowl, add the ground almonds, and replace any bran sifted from the flour. Line a 20 cm (8 in) round or 18 cm (7 in) square tin with greaseproof paper and wipe the paper with rapeseed oil.

Mix the sugar and prune purée together in a large mixing bowl and beat in the black treacle. Add the eggs in stages, beating thoroughly after each addition. Fold in the flour mixture and the dried fruit mixture alternately, a little at a time, beating well until all the ingredients are thoroughly mixed. Transfer the mixture into the prepared tin and smooth the top with the back of a wetted metal spoon. Bake in the oven at 150 °C (300 °F, gas 2) for 3 hours or until cooked through.

To test, insert a clean metal skewer into the middle of the cake: if the skewer comes out clean, the cake is cooked; if there are smears of mixture on the skewer, cook the cake for a further 15 minutes before testing again. If the cake becomes dark on top before it is cooked through, lay a piece of foil loosely over the tin and complete the cooking. Once cooked, leave the cake to cool in the tin for about 1 hour before turning it out onto a wire rack to cool completely.

Glossary

amino acid A chemical compound containing nitrogen and carbon which can be joined with other amino acids to make a protein. When protein is digested, it is broken down into amino acids.

anaphylaxis A rare, life-threatening allergic reaction involving breathing difficulty and a drop in blood pressure (shock).

anorexia nervosa An eating disorder, most often affecting teenage girls and young women, in which altered body image and fear of gaining weight can lead to dangerous weight loss.

antioxidants Helpful substances such as vitamins C and E that protect against the damaging effects of free radicals. Fruits and vegetables are rich sources of antioxidants.

artery A blood vessel that carries blood *away* from the heart.

aspartame An intense sweetener (E951), used in tiny quantities as a sugar substitute.

benzoic acid A food preservative (E210) to which a small minority of children appear to be sensitive.

bulimia   An eating disorder involving bouts of binge eating and self-induced vomiting.

calorie   A unit of heat. The number of 'calories per 100 g' of a food is a measure of the energy supplied by the food. This actually refers to kilocalories and should really be written with a capital C; one Calorie or kilocalorie equals 1000 calories.

casein   A protein found in milk curds.

CHD   Coronary heart disease.

cholesterol   A fatty substance found in animals and people but not in plants. High levels of cholesterol in the blood increase the risk of heart disease.

coeliac disease   An uncommon condition in which the intestine is sensitive to gluten (wheat protein) resulting in poor absorption of nutrients from food. To stay well, sufferers have to avoid gluten.

coronary heart disease   Heart disease resulting from a build-up of fatty deposits in the coronary arteries which supply blood to the heart; it may cause angina, a heart attack or sudden death. This sort of heart disease is so much more common than any other kind that it is often called simply 'heart disease'.

curds   The lumps that form in milk when the whey separates, for example during cheese-making.

diabetes (diabetes mellitus)   The medical condition in which blood glucose levels rise because the body is either not producing enough of the hormone insulin (type 1 diabetes) or not responding properly to it (type 2 diabetes).

diuretic   A drug that stimulates production of urine.

E number   An identification number given to a food additive approved throughout the European Union.

essential amino acid   An amino acid that cannot be made by the body and must be obtained from food.

essential fatty acid A fatty acid that needs to be obtained from food because the body is unable to make it.

failure to thrive Failure of a baby or toddler to grow at the expected rate.

faltering growth Another name for 'failure to thrive'.

fatty acids The chemical units that make up fat.

food allergy Sensitivity to a particular food substance, such as a protein in cows' milk, arising from overreaction of the body's immune system. Resulting symptoms may be mild (e.g. itchy skin) or severe (e.g. anaphylaxis).

food intolerance A tendency to be upset by a particular food, such as milk, which may not involve the immune system. For example, people with lactose intolerance cannot digest milk properly; they are not allergic to milk but they get diarrhoea when they drink it.

free radicals Unstable chemicals that damage body tissues (by a process called 'oxidation') contributing to the development of heart disease and cancer. Antioxidants, for example from fruit and vegetables, help to protect us against free radical attack.

GI Glycaemic index.

gluten Protein found in wheat, rye and certain other grains. Food given to babies under six months should be gluten-free.

glycaemic index A number indicating how fast the carbohydrate in a food is converted to blood glucose.

HBV protein High biological value protein.

HDL-cholesterol High-density lipoprotein cholesterol. Cholesterol in this form is being transported away from artery walls. It is often called 'good cholesterol' because the higher the level of HDL-cholesterol, the lower the risk of heart disease.

high biological value protein A protein containing adequate amounts of all the essential amino acids. Most plant proteins, unlike animal proteins, are 'low biological value proteins' and need to be combined with other foods to make up for missing amino acids.

hoummos (hummus) Puréed chickpeas, mixed with tahini, oil, lemon and garlic.

hydrogenated vegetable oil Vegetable oil that has been chemically altered during food processing to make it less runny; it should be regarded as saturated fat and avoided as much as possible.

LDL-cholesterol Low-density lipoprotein cholesterol. Most of the cholesterol in the blood is in this form. It can form fatty deposits on artery walls; a raised level of LDL-cholesterol in the blood means a higher risk of heart disease.

monosodium glutamate A food additive frequently used as a flavour enhancer. Like ordinary salt, sodium chloride, it raises the sodium content of food; there is a link between high-sodium diets and high blood pressure.

mono-unsaturated fatty acids (mono-unsaturates) Fatty acids in which only one area of the molecule is not saturated with hydrogen; olive oil and rapeseed oil contain high levels of mono-unsaturates. Replacing saturated fat in the diet with mono-unsaturates is good for the heart and arteries.

omega-3 (n-3) fatty acids Polyunsaturated fatty acids, particularly abundant in fish oils, that are good for the circulation.

omega-6 (n-6) fatty acids Polyunsaturated fatty acids found in vegetable oils such as sunflower and corn oils.

Parmesan A hard Italian cheese.

pecorino An Italian cheese similar to Parmesan. A little grated pecorino can add a lot of flavour, but large quantities will add a lot of salt too.

polyunsaturated fatty acids (polyunsaturates) Fatty acids in which more than one area of the molecule is not saturated with hydrogen; they are abundant in vegetable oils and nuts. Replacing saturates in the diet with polyunsaturates lowers blood cholesterol.

quark A soft cheese made from skimmed milk – a very useful ingredient in all sorts of recipes, rather than a cheese to be eaten by itself.

Quorn A low-fat, high-protein meat substitute made from a fungus (like mushroom) and egg white. It has a chicken-like texture and takes on the flavour of the sauce it is cooked in.

RDA Recommended daily amount (or, in America, 'recommended dietary allowance').

recommended daily amount The daily intake of a vitamin, mineral or other nutrient needed to prevent deficiency. Although this term is still widely used, nutritionists often refer to 'reference nutrient intake' (RNI).

roux A mixture of flour and fat, heated together and used to make a sauce.

saccharin An artificial sweetener (E954), used instead of sugar to add sweetness without calories.

saturated fatty acids (saturates) Fatty acids in which the molecule has no room for any more hydrogen atoms; they occur particularly in animal fat (but also in palm oil and coconut). A diet high in saturates raises blood cholesterol levels.

skimmed milk Milk from which the fat has been removed; it still contains just as much calcium and protein as whole milk. Semi-skimmed milk has had half the fat removed.

sorbitol A sweetener used in some products as an alternative to sugar; large quantities cause stomach cramps and diarrhoea.

stanols Substances derived from sterols; like plant sterols, stanols can be added to fatty foods (such as fat spreads) to reduce absorption of cholesterol from the intestine.

sterols Naturally occurring compounds related to cholesterol – a sterol found in animals but not in plants. Plant sterols can be added to a fat spread to lower blood cholesterol by reducing cholesterol absorption in the intestine.

stock A broth produced by simmering meat, poultry, fish, bones or vegetables and used as an ingredient in soups, casseroles and other dishes.

stroke Damage to part of the brain caused by haemorrhage or blockage of an artery. The consequences depend on the area of the brain affected and often include reduced movement on one side of the body and speech difficulties.

tahini (tahina) A paste made from ground sesame seeds.

tartrazine A food colouring agent (E102) commonly used in soft drinks.

thrombosis The formation of a blood clot within the circulation.

tofu Soya bean curd. It is a useful alternative to meat and an ingredient in many recipes.

trans fatty acids Chemically altered fatty acids found particularly in hard margarines and hydrogenated vegetable oil. They are bad for arteries and best avoided.

tzatziki A Greek dip made with yoghurt, cucumber and garlic.

urticaria A rash, also known as hives or nettle rash, in which itchy weals appear on the skin. The cause is often unknown, but it is sometimes triggered by an allergic reaction to food.

vegan A person who avoids eating any foods of animal origin.

vegetarian Someone who avoids eating meat and, perhaps, other foods of animal origin. A lacto-vegetarian includes milk in the diet; a lacto-ovo-vegetarian includes milk and eggs.

vein   A blood vessel that returns blood *to* the heart.

whey   The watery part of mik that separates from the curds.

Further information

Organisations

Parentalk
PO Box 23142
London SE1 0ZT

Tel: 0700 2000 500
Fax: 020 7450 9060
e-mail: info@parentalk.co.uk
Web site: www.parentalk.co.uk

Provides a range of resources and services designed to inspire parents to enjoy parenthood.

British Allergy Foundation
Deepdene House
30 Bellgrove Road
Wellington
Kent DA16 3PY

Helpline: 020 8303 8583
Tel: 020 8303 8525

e-mail: allergybaf@compuserve.com
Web site: www.allergyfoundation
.com

Provides information on allergies, including food allergies.

British Dental Health Foundation
Eastlands Court
St Peter's Road
Rugby
Warwickshire CV21 3QP

Tel: 01788 546356
Fax: 01788 541982
e-mail: feedback@dentalhealth.org
.uk
Web site: www.dentalhealth.org.uk

Aims to promote the benefits of achieving and maintaining the highest standards of dental health.

British Heart Foundation
14 Fitzhardinge Street
London W1H 6DH

Tel: 020 7935 0185
Fax: 020 7486 5820
Web site: www.bhf.org.uk

Educates the public and health professionals about heart disease prevention and treatment.

British Nutrition Foundation
High Holborn House
52–54 High Holborn
London WC1V 6RQ

Tel: 020 7404 6504
Fax: 020 7404 6747
e-mail: postbox@nutrition.org.uk
Web site: www.nutrition.org.uk

Promotes the nutritional well-being of the population.

Child Growth Foundation
2 Mayfield Avenue
Chiswick
London W4 1PW

Tel: 020 8994 7625

Produces growth charts and provides information for parents concerned about their child's growth.

Diabetes UK
10 Queen Anne Street
London W1G 9LH

Tel: 020 7323 1531
Fax: 020 7637 3644

e-mail: info@diabetes.org.uk
Web site: www.diabetes.org.uk

Provides help and support to people with diabetes and supports diabetes research.

Eating Disorder Association
First Floor, Wensum House
103 Prince of Wales Road
Norwich NR1 1DW

Helpline: 01603 621414 (weekdays
    9.00 a.m.–6.30 p.m.)
Youthline: 01603 765050
    (weekdays 4.00–6.00 p.m.)
e-mail: info@edauk.com
Web site: www.edauk.com

Provides advice and information on eating problems to both sufferers and their families.

Food Directory
Tel: 020 7388 7421
Fax: 020 7388 7761
e-mail: foodfoundation@btinternet
    .com
Web site: www.fooddirectory.co.uk

The Food Directory has been established by The Food Foundation, a registered charity established to advance the education and awareness of the public, in particular young people, about the benefits of sound nutrition, cooking and other food skills, and the use and appreciation of food and drink.

La Lèche League
(Great Britain)
BM 3424
London WC1N 3XX

Tel: 020 7242 1278

Helps women who want to breast-feed. You can send a SAE for details of your nearest counsellor or group.

National Childbirth Trust (NCT)
Alexandra House
Oldham Terrace
London W3 6NH

Tel: 0870 444 8707
Breastfeeding line: 0870 444 8708

Provides support for breastfeeding mothers as well as information on antenatal classes and postnatal groups.

Thinkfast
Web site: www.thinkfast.co.uk

The Thinkfast web site was produced by the Health Education Authority and is aimed at anyone, particularly those between the ages of 15 and 34, who eats fast food. It aims to help people choose a health-ier diet and reduce the rates of coronary heart disease.

Vegan Society
Donald Wilson House
7 Battle Road
St Leonards-on-Sea
East Sussex TN37 7AA

Tel: 01424 427393

If you would like information, send a large SAE.

Vegetarian Society
Parkdale
Dunham Road
Altrincham
Cheshire WA14 4QG

Tel: 0161 928 0793
e-mail: info@vegsoc.org
Web site: www.vegsoc.org

You can send a SAE to obtain a list of local groups.

General Parenting Organisations

Care for the Family
PO Box 488
Cardiff CF15 7YY

Tel: 029 2081 0800
Fax: 029 2081 4089
e-mail: care.for.the.family@cff.org
.uk
Web site: www.care-for-the-family
.org.uk

Provides support for families through seminars, resources and special projects.

Fathers Direct
Tamarisk House
37 The Tele Village
Crickhowell
Powys NP8 1BP

Tel: 01873 810515
Web site: www.fathersdirect.com

An information resource for fathers.

Gingerbread
16–17 Clerkenwell Close
London EC1R 0AA

Tel: 020 7336 8183
Fax: 020 7336 8185
e-mail: office@gingerbread.org.uk
Web site: www.gingerbread.org.uk

Provides day-to-day support and practical help for lone parents.

National Council for One Parent Families
255 Kentish Town Road
London NW5 2LX

Lone Parent Line: 0800 018 5026
Maintenance & Money Line: 020 7428 5424
(Mon & Fri 10.30 a.m.–1.30 p.m.; Wed 3–6 p.m.)

An information service for lone parents.

National Family and Parenting Institute
430 Highgate Studios
53–79 Highgate Road
London NW5 1TL

Tel: 020 7424 3460
Fax: 020 7485 3590

e-mail: info@nfpi.org
Web site: www.nfpi.org

An independent charity set up to provide a strong national focus on parenting and families in the twenty-first century.

NSPCC
NSPCC National Centre
42 Curtain Road
London EC2A 3NH

Helpline: 0800 800 500
Tel: 020 7825 2500
Fax: 020 7825 2525
Web site: www.nspcc.org.uk

Aims to prevent child abuse and neglect in all its forms and give practical help to families with children at risk. The NSPCC also produces leaflets with information and advice on positive parenting – for these, call 020 7825 2500.

Parentline Plus
520 Highgate Studios
53–76 Highgate Road
Kentish Town
London NW5 1TL

Helpline: 0808 800 2222
Textphone: 0800 783 6783
Fax: 020 7284 5501
e-mail: centraloffice@parentline plus.org.uk
Web site: www.parentlineplus.org .uk

Provides a freephone helpline called Parentline and courses for parents via the Parent Network Service. Parentline Plus also includes the National Stepfamily Association. For all information, call the Parentline freephone number: 0808 800 2222.

Positive Parenting
1st Floor
2A South Street
Gosport PO12 1ES

Tel: 023 9252 8787
Fax: 023 9250 1111
e-mail: info@parenting.org.uk
Web site: www.parenting.org.uk

Aims to prepare people for the role of parenting by helping parents, those about to become parents and also those who lead parenting groups.

Relate: National Marriage Guidance
National Headquarters
Herbert Gray College
Little Church Street
Rugby
Warwickshire CV21 3AP

Tel: 01788 573241
Fax: 01788 535007
e-mail: enquiries@national.relate
  .org.uk
Web site: www.relate.org.uk

Parenting Courses

- **Parentalk Parenting Course**
  A new parenting course designed to give parents the opportunity to share their experiences, learn from each other and discover some principles of parenting.

  Parentalk
  PO Box 23142
  London SE1 0ZT

  For more information, phone 0700 2000 500

- **Positive Parenting**
  Publishes a range of low-cost, easy-to-read, common-sense resource materials which provide help, information and advice. Responsible for running a range of parenting courses across the UK. For more information, phone 023 9252 8787.

- **Parent Network**
  For more information, call Parentline Plus on 0808 800 2222.

The **Paren**✝alk Parenting Course

Helping you to be a Better Parent

Being a parent is not easy. **Parentalk** is a new, video-led, parenting course designed to give groups of parents the opportunity to share their experiences, learn from each other and discover some principles of parenting. It is suitable for anyone who is a parent or is planning to become a parent.

The Parentalk Parenting Course features:

Steve Chalke – TV Presenter; author on parenting and family issues; father of four and **Parentalk** Chairman.
Rob Parsons – author of *The Sixty Minute Father* and *The Sixty Minute Mother*; and Executive Director of Care for the Family.
Dr Caroline Dickinson – inner city-based GP and specialist in obstetrics, gynaecology and paediatrics.
Kate Robbins – well-known actress and comedienne.

Each **Parentalk** session is packed with group activities and discussion starters.

Made up of eight sessions, the **Parentalk** Parenting Course is easy to use and includes everything you need to host a group of up to ten parents.

Each Parentalk Course Pack contains:
- A **Parentalk** video
- Extensive, easy-to-use, group leader's guide
- Ten copies of the full-colour course material for members
- Photocopiable sheets/OHP masters

Price £49.95

Additional participant materials are available so that the course can be run again and again.

To order your copy, or to find out more, please contact:

Paren✝alk
PO Box 23142, London SE1 0ZT
Tel: 0700 2000 500
Fax: 020 7450 9060
e-mail: info@parentalk.co.uk